Exploring Character

**Real Life Scenarios That Will
Get Students Talking about
Values, Choices, and Behavior**

R. E. Myers

A
GOOD
YEAR
BOOK™

Dedication

To Kathleen, with love and admiration.

Good Year Books

Are available for most basic curriculum subjects plus many enrichment areas. For more Good Year Books, contact your local bookseller or educational dealer. For a complete catalog with information about other Good Year Books, please contact:

Good Year Books
P.O. Box 91858
Tucson, AZ 85752-1858
www.goodyearbooks.com

Cover design: Gary Smith, Performance Design
Text design: Doug Goewey
Drawings: Sean O'Neill
Cover photos: comstock.com

ISBN-10: 1-59647-057-7
ISBN-13: 978-1-59647-057-6
1 2 3 4 5 6 7 8 9 10 – MG – 09 08 07 06

Contents

Kindness

Trustworthiness

Contents

Introduction

You'll often hear people talk about character and the important role that schools play in teaching students about good character traits. In fact, many adults appear to feel that schools bear a major responsibility for teaching our youth such concepts as trustworthiness, loyalty, respect, honesty, and courage. This notion is hardly radical because in every society adults have tried to inculcate the values they deem most important in young people. Moreover, the idea is practical, because how our students regard these concepts affects everything they do in school and out of school—from cheating with the aid of electronics, to engaging in a riot at a football game, to participating in programs for the needy.

These days students have an enormous number of choices to make, and making those choices is the means of developing character. Like it or not, teachers must deal with the choices their students are making. By discussing in class the dilemmas that students face, your students will become better able to make the right choices. What follows is an attempt to involve your students in thinking seriously about the elements that make up the character of a responsible individual in our society.

How to Use This Book

Each of the units in this book is meant to stimulate in-depth discussion of one or more dilemmas. Accordingly, what's most important is what happens after your students read the story and then reflect on it.

There are three ways that you can present a story. You can read it to the class. Your students can read it silently on their own. Or you can have one or more of your students read it to the class. In choosing one of the three procedures, you should consider the story's relevance to your students' lives and its probable impact upon them.

Whichever way you choose to present the story, it is important that you set the stage properly. A certain amount of warm-up is necessary if you want students in the mood to think about subjects such as cheating, being fair, and trying hard. You can bring up the subject by citing a newspaper article or a personal anecdote, or you can simply make a remark or ask a question that leads in to the topic.

An activity or exercise follows each story. These activities are intended as a way to get students talking about the ideas and issues brought out by the story. This will provoke your students into deeper thinking, and some of the thinking will bring forth insights.

You do not have to teach the units in any particular order, and you do not need to teach every unit. Please select only those units that are most pertinent or topical to your students, so they gain a better understanding of what having good character means and how they display good character in their choices, actions, and attitudes. And, by all means, feel free to modify anything in this book that will make it more appropriate for your students.

The Broken Blade

Gary decided to make a metal box to give to his father on his birthday. He didn't have very many tools at home, and so he asked his friend Luke if he could borrow a couple of his tools to finish up the box. Luke told him to come around any time and use the tools he had in the little shop that his father had in the garage. So one Saturday Gary went over to Luke's house, which was only two blocks away. He rang the doorbell to let Luke or his parents know he was going to use the tools in the shop. No one was at home, and so Gary went into the shop and found a hacksaw he needed to cut off a part of the box. After some strenuous sawing, Gary was surprised and appalled that the blade of the hacksaw snapped.

More than anything, Gary was embarrassed because he hadn't used the tool properly. He didn't know what to do. There were no other hacksaw blades around the shop that he could see. He decided the best course of action would be to go to the hardware store and buy a hacksaw blade. And that is what he did. When he returned to Luke's shop with a hacksaw blade, he replaced the broken one and tucked it into his shirt. Then he finished work on the box and quickly went home.

On Monday, at school, Luke asked Gary if he had been able to come over and work on that box. Gary stammered a bit, and then said that he had and thanked Luke for the use of the hacksaw. When he replaced the broken blade, he had noticed that the one he bought wasn't exactly the same as the original one. He wondered if Luke or his father would notice. Gary was too embarrassed about the incident to tell Luke what had happened. He made a remark about playing baseball after school and then got away.

Name _____   Date _____

The Broken Blade: Student Responses

Think about your answers to the following questions and write your response to each.

1. Should Gary keep quiet about the broken hacksaw blade, or should he tell Luke the next time he sees him?

_____

_____

2. Hacksaw blades aren't hard to break if you are inexperienced in using the tool. Do you think Luke knows this and wouldn't think much about the incident?

_____

_____

3. Do you think it was silly of Gary to be so embarrassed at breaking the blade? Explain.

_____

_____

_____

4. What would you have done if you were Gary?

_____

_____

_____

The Broken Blade
Truthfulness

The Story

The problem of "owning up" to our mistakes is a serious and recurrent one. Teachers learn early that trying to cover up a mistake in front of a class makes matters worse. Teachers don't have to be infallible know-it-alls, and students don't expect them to be. Similarly, admitting a mistake is very difficult for some young people. Gary was one of these. He was embarrassed at having been given the privilege of using some hand tools by his friend and then breaking the blade of the hacksaw he was using. He didn't know it then, but most likely Luke or his father had broken a blade not too long before. Accomplished craftsmen don't break them, but ordinary do-it-yourselfers do. At any rate, Gary tried to cover up his misadventure with the hacksaw. He was apprehensive about being found out and had a guilty conscience.

Only by having experiences of this kind as they mature will students realize that confessing to a mistake and being truthful about the incident is much easier than covering up. Most of your students should have had an experience similar to Gary's, and you might gently encourage them to offer analogous anecdotes.

The Questions

The first question has to do with the wisdom of telling or not telling Luke about the broken blade. The majority of your students will see the advantages of Gary's confessing that he had broken the blade and replaced it. Most of them will probably think that replacing the blade made everything all right. Challenge them about this point, however. If replacing the blade made everything all right, why was Gary so reluctant to tell Luke about the incident?

The second question invites your students to conjecture about the frequency with which hacksaw blades get broken. A few of your students may have some knowledge about hand tools that they can share.

The third question gets at the heart of the problem: Why was Gary so embarrassed by his breaking the blade? Is he an average, ordinary boy, or is he especially sensitive and perhaps proud? Maybe he's just someone who hates very much to be in the wrong.

The last question might best be answered in private so that the student can give an honest answer. Many of your students will be eager to give their opinion about how they would have handled the incident, however, and some will be frank to say that Gary is probably a "wimp."

For the Teacher

An Activity Exploring Truthfulness

The activity following the story allows your students to probe more deeply into Gary's problem and its ramifications. "Stretching It," on page 7, explores the use of half-truths and falsehoods in writing and speaking to the public. It addresses the purposes of the fiction writer as well as those of the propagandist and apologist. In public life a very great amount of soul-searching and finger-pointing is often conducted under the banner of "revealing the truth." Are there times when the public should be told falsehoods, or are there other times when it is better if the public doesn't know the entire truth?

The key word in "Stretching It" is *lying*. How your students interpret the word will have a lot to do with how they react to the seven situations presented, all of which have some dubious and/or devious verbal responses. One or two of the seven situations may hit home. Hopefully, your students will recognize these commonplace instances of avoiding telling the truth.

This is how a strict judging of the truthfulness of the seven responses might be interpreted:

1. Embellishing a story is a mild kind of lying because it isn't being completely factual. It's a form of exaggerating, but because it isn't truthful, we can say it is lying.

2. Omitting critical facts falls in the area of misrepresentation or dishonesty. It isn't lying. Nevertheless, the intent is very close.

3. Shifting the blame to another person is dishonorable and reprehensible, but it isn't exactly lying.

4. "What pie?" is evasive and very much like lying when the person asking the question is guilty of eating that pie. Strictly speaking, it isn't lying.

5. Changing the subject slightly is a common tactic employed by people who want to avoid telling the truth, but it isn't lying.

6. "Uh-huh" translates to "Yes," and so it is lying.

7. Obviously, giving a false age is lying, no matter how old the individual is.

After the students have each responded, hold a class discussion of your students' reactions. Point out that in each case an individual wants to avoid telling the truth. That generalization shouldn't escape any of your students.

Name   Date

What Pie?

Stretching It

An activity about truthfulness

Write *yes* or *no* on the line at the left of each of the descriptions, depending upon whether you think the situation is an instance of lying or not. Under each item, give the reasons for your decision. You'll have to have a good definition of the word *lie*. After additional thought, you may decide to change a *yes* to a *no*, or vice versa.

Are you really lying if you:

_____ **1.** Add a couple of details to a humorous anecdote that aren't strictly true?

_____

_____

_____

_____ **2.** Omit only one fact that would show your responsibility when you tell how you lost your front-door key?

_____

_____

_____

ACTIVITY

From *Exploring Character*, Copyright © Good Year Books. This page may be reproduced for classroom use only by the actual purchaser of the book. www.goodyearbooks.com.

Name   **Date**

_____ **3.** Emphasize another person's role in an escapade when questioned by your very upset parents?

_____

_____

_____

_____ **4.** Mumble "What pie?" when asked what happened to the piece of pie you ate an hour ago?

_____

_____

_____

_____ **5.** Evade a question about what happened to a lamp you broke while tossing a ball in the living room?

_____

_____

_____

_____ **6.** Answer with a muffled "Uh-huh" when you are asked if you did a chore that you didn't do?

_____

_____

_____

_____ **7.** Say you are older than you really are to get into a movie?

_____

_____

_____

Pedro's Dilemma

It was one of those times when a young person didn't quite know what to do. The teacher, who was known to become confused upon occasion, had gotten Pepper and Pedro mixed up. She had asked Pedro to represent the school at the youth conference next month. That meant going to the state capitol for two days, and Pedro wouldn't mind getting out of school and maybe having some fun. Pedro knew that her intention was to designate Pepper Ramos, who was absent with the flu, as the school's representative. The two of them were about the same size, and they were always together.

He mumbled something to Ms. Ortiz after she had told him of the honor, and then she moved away from his desk to answer a question in the back of the classroom. Well, there really wasn't any doubt about it. Even though Ms. Ortiz had given him the packet for the conference, Pedro would have to go up to her desk when she came back to it and let her know she'd made a mistake. Quite a few people had called

Pedro "Pepper" and vice versa. It wasn't especially surprising that Ms. Ortiz had mixed them up. Ms. Ortiz would have discovered her mistake before long anyway, but Pedro thought he shouldn't hang on to the packet. Pepper was the one who deserved to go. The trouble was, he didn't like to embarrass Ms. Ortiz.

"Uhh, Ms. Ortiz," started Pedro hesitantly, "I don't think you want me to have this. It must be for Pepper. He's not here today. Pepper is the kind of student who should represent our school. I'd like to go, but Pepper is the one you want."

"What? Oh my! Have I confused you two again?" said Ms. Ortiz. "I'm sorry. You're Pedro, aren't you? Thank you, Pedro." In a way, Ms. Ortiz was sorry that it wasn't Pedro who was going to the conference.

_____   _____
Name   **Date**

Pedro's Dilemma: Student Responses

Think about your answers to the following questions and write your response to each.

1. Because Ms. Ortiz was certain to discover her mistake sooner or later, was Pedro's pointing out her error just a matter of cutting short the time when he'd be feeling guilty, or was it an indication of his honesty?

_____

_____

2. Confusing the faces of people who look alike is a common mistake. Have you ever had it happen to you? Describe the situation.

_____

_____

_____

_____

3. If people do the "right thing" in cases such as this, is it because they figure they will get found out anyway?

_____

_____

4. What did Ms. Ortiz mean when she thought about being sorry Pedro wasn't the one going to the conference?

_____

_____

For the Teacher

Pedro's Dilemma
Honesty

The Story

Although the virtue set forth in this story is honesty, we haven't made it the kind of honesty in which someone chases down a person who has just dropped a wallet or purse. Pedro's decision to let Ms. Ortiz know that he wasn't the intended recipient of the honor wasn't really long in coming. He realized that the mistake in identity would be revealed in a day or two at most. Pedro endeared himself to Ms. Ortiz because he was so open about the fact that Pepper deserved the honor far more than he did.

The Questions

Your students may very well think that Pedro didn't have much choice about calling the teacher's attention to the mistake and that his behavior is nothing special. The point about his wanting to cut short a time in which he'd feel funny about having the packet may prompt them to think about the times we're honest because we don't want to feel guilty.

You might wish to have a brief discussion of the failing some of us have in confusing people because of similarities in their faces, builds, heights, mannerisms, clothing, and the like. It's the cause of severe embarrassment at times, and about all the advice you can give someone who is prone to misidentifying people is to try to remember to be a little cautious where there is any doubt.

The most searching of any of the four questions has to do with our being honest because we're bound to be found out anyway. Is fear of exposure one of the main reasons we do the honest thing much of the time? When the odds are very good that we'll get caught, it's easier to be honest. Right?

Pedro's consideration for Ms. Ortiz is perhaps more noteworthy than his promptly telling her of her mistake. That was probably why she was a little sorry that it wasn't Pedro who was going to the conference.

An Activity Exploring Honesty

The activity "It's a Shame!" on page 13 examines the relationship between embarrassment, shame, and honesty. Before the exercise ask students whether they would take an apple off a tree in someone's front yard if there were absolutely no chance of being caught. Would they take the risk of being seen stealing the apple if there was a chance of someone, such as the owner of the property, seeing them? Would it make any difference how hungry they were? Then distribute the handout. Follow up with a discussion of students' responses.

Name   Date

It's a Shame!

An activity exploring honesty

Write your answers on the lines below.

When should people be ashamed?
Should they ever be ashamed of other
people who associated with them?
Explain.

_____

_____

_____

What is the difference between shame and embarrassment?

_____

_____

Does shame come mainly when you are caught doing something wrong,
or can you feel as much shame even if you aren't caught?

_____

_____

_____

Would you be ashamed if you:

1. were caught stealing $1.00? Explain.

_____

_____

2. were caught stealing $50.00? Explain.

_____

_____

ACTIVITY

Name   **Date**

3. stole $1.00 but weren't caught? Explain.

_____

_____

4. stole $25.00 but weren't caught? Explain.

_____

_____

5. lied about what you did when asked by a parent or guardian and were found out? Explain.

_____

_____

6. came to school without a lunch—or money to buy a lunch—and had to borrow money to buy lunch? Explain.

_____

_____

7. had to go to a party dressed in clothes that weren't nearly as nice as everyone else's? Explain.

_____

_____

8. made an error in a game that allowed the other team to win? Explain.

_____

_____

9. cheated on an exam and were caught? Explain.

_____

_____

10. cheated on an exam and weren't caught? Explain.

_____

_____

Wayward Ants

Thomas knew that half of his grade in Miss Fulton's science class depended upon a report about ants. Miss Fulton had given the same assignment for 15 years, but she specified that each student tackle it in his or her own way and without working with any other student. The problem, as Miss Fulton posed it, was: "What happens to ants that you inadvertently bring home after you've had a picnic at a park or in the country? Do they join ants in another colony or do they forage for themselves?" The catch was that at least half of the report had to deal with the actual tracking of the ants. Miss Fulton was considered eccentric by her students.

In spite of some anxiety regarding his grade, Thomas had put off working on the report for several weeks. Now there were only two days left before the report was to be handed in (*no* reports would be accepted after class on Monday!), and Thomas hadn't trailed an ant. He happened to be looking in the attic for an old baseball glove that Saturday when he came upon a box of drawings, report cards, and papers that his brother James, who was 10 years older than Thomas, had saved. Thomas idly shuffled through the memorabilia when, lo and behold, he came upon a report about relocated ants! James had been a good student and he'd done a fine job of tracking ants for Miss Fulton 10 years ago. Would she remember that report from all of the hundreds that had been submitted to her over the years? Thomas tended to doubt it, but you never knew about Miss Fulton. Anyway, this find was an answer to a dimly felt prayer. He'd copy the report James had labored over those many years ago and be assured of a good grade. "I'm home free!" thought Thomas.

RESPONSES

From *Exploring Character*, Copyright © Good Year Books. This page may be reproduced for classroom use only by the actual purchaser of the book. www.goodyearbooks.com.

Name   Date

Wayward Ants: Student Responses

Think about your answers to the following questions and write your response to each.

1. Do you think Thomas got away with turning in a copy of his brother's report? If not, would Miss Fulton think that Thomas had cheated in the same way that she would if she had caught him looking over someone's shoulder during a test?

_____

_____

_____

2. Is taking someone else's work and claiming credit for it stealing? What is the word people use for doing that?

_____

3. What else could Thomas have done in order to write a decent report about the ants?

_____

_____

_____

4. Is stealing from your brother different from stealing someone's work in a book or on the Internet?

_____

_____

Wayward Ants
Dishonesty

The Story

How your students react to this little story is problematic, depending upon the current ethos among their peers regarding cheating and similar offenses. Many will weigh in against Thomas's act because they think they are supposed to respond that way. After all, this story was read and reacted to in class. Others may be more openly sympathetic to Thomas. Haven't we all procrastinated at one time or another?

In the spring of 2002 a brouhaha about high school students in Kansas plagiarizing material from the Internet opened the eyes of a great many people. A biology teacher had assigned a report about leaves. She later gave zeroes to twenty-eight of her students who were caught lifting material from the Internet for their reports—after signing a document before the term that stated cheating would not be tolerated. Their parents pressured the school board into softening the punishment, resulting in the teacher quitting her job. As syndicated columnist Leonard Pitts put it, the teacher "went to school the next day [after the parents had besieged the school board members] and found the kids in a celebratory mood, cheering their victory and crowing that they no longer had to listen to teachers." Coincidentally, two famous historians were also found to have plagiarized material at about the same time, thus worsening the case for honesty among young people.

Because students have always cheated, and are more likely to do so as the pressures upon them increase, why shouldn't Thomas be excused of his indiscretion? The answer is, as columnist Leonard Pitts, Jr., pointed out, "Reputation . . . is about who you are when people are watching. Character is about who you are when there's nobody in the room but you. Both matter, but of the two, character is far and away the most important."

The Questions

If your students "buy" the story about Thomas and his purloined report—and some cynical ones might not—their first thought might be: "Did he get away with it?" Miss Fulton seems like the kind of teacher who would recognize a duplicate report, even though it had been ten years since she'd read it.

The next question has to do with the word *stealing*. There is a mild request for the student to identify "Thomas's" behavior as plagiarism. The word is not used in the story.

For the Teacher

Your students are asked what else Thomas could have done to turn in a decent report. Well, he could at least have read up about ants and perhaps consulted someone who knew about them. He could have made an attempt to capture a few ants in a park and relocate them in his yard. Surely two days was enough time in which to carry out that part of the assignment.

Finally, the question of whether it is okay to copy from a brother's paper brings the plagiarism problem into sharper focus. It isn't any more legitimate to copy a relative's paper than that of a stranger, because it is the *act* of copying that is wrong.

An Activity Exploring Dishonesty

Some of the dozen deceptions given in the activity are harmless and don't injure anyone, but others are practices that are either dishonest in a legal sense or just barely legal. The Better Business Bureau and the Office for Consumer Affairs are very much concerned with fraudulent and deceptive practices by individuals and firms. With the advent of the Internet, scams and dishonest schemes have burgeoned.

This activity could be just the prelude to a unit about this topic if you and your class should find it worthwhile. At a minimum, "Is It Dishonest, Illegal, or Just Fun?" on page 19 will alert your students to the nearly endless machinations of unscrupulous persons who greatly desire to separate gullible people from their money. Seniors in particular have been targeted by bunco artists who present investment schemes, hit-and-run home repairs, and fraudulent deals to these vulnerable people. Your students should be made aware of these deceptions early in their lives.

Name   **Date**

Is It Dishonest, Illegal, or Just Fun?

An activity exploring dishonesty

Buying a building lot from a real estate developer by looking at an artist's drawings of what the community will look like (perhaps) on a computer screen is taking a decided risk. Is the developer misrepresenting this opportunity? It's hard to tell. At the very least, buying a lot would be a gamble for anyone.

There are many people engaged in fraudulent activities throughout the country. Others practice deceptions that are only slightly illegal. Many more deceive people in a harmless way. Below are other instances of individuals deceiving others. Decide whether these actions are actually illegal, dishonest but not exactly illegal, or harmless, and then tell why you think so.

1. A stage magician apparently saws a young lady in half before your unbelieving eyes.

_____

_____

2. The owner of a health club/gymnasium promises you a "new body" if you will enroll as a member.

_____

_____

3. An ad for a perfume promises "enchanting nights" and "irresistible allure" to the purchaser.

_____

_____

4. A mystery story writer gives many false clues before revealing the murderer at the end of the book.

_____

_____

ACTIVITY

Name   Date

5. A used car dealer puts sawdust in the crankcase of an older car to make the engine run more smoothly.

_____

_____

6. A short man wears "elevator" shoes to make him appear taller.

_____

_____

7. An ad for a weight-loss pill guarantees the loss of 10 pounds in a month if you will take it daily.

_____

_____

8. An ad for a ring "featuring a precious stone" declares that it is "free," but there are substantial fees and shipping charges given in very small print at the bottom of the ad.

_____

_____

9. A person running for office promises to cut taxes for everyone during a time of high inflation throughout the country.

_____

_____

10. Questionable accounting practices show a profit for a corporation when there was actually an operating loss.

_____

_____

Cheater!

Tanya winced. And then she looked to her right. Eddie was at it again, peaking over at her paper. This was a final test in math, and Tanya was nervous. Now she had to contend with Eddie, who was known among his classmates as someone who didn't mind using other people's ideas. Eddie would cheat on tests by writing on his desk, shirt sleeve, or his pant leg. If he could, Eddie would also look over the shoulder of anyone he thought would have the right answers.

Ordinarily Tanya would have just been annoyed with Eddie, but on this occasion she was really irritated because she was having a hard time concentrating on the problems.

After the test was over, Tanya got together with Becky at recess. She was still very unhappy.

"I can't stand that Eddie! Nobody likes him," asserted Tanya.

"You can't respect a cheater," said Becky.

RESPONSES

From *Exploring Character*, Copyright © Good Year Books. This page may be reproduced for classroom use only by the actual purchaser of the book. www.goodyearbooks.com.

Name   **Date**

Cheater!: Student Responses

Think about your answers to the following questions and write your
response to each.

1. Do you think Eddie cared if people disliked him? Tell why or why not.

_____

_____

_____

_____

2. Didn't Eddie want other students to respect him? What else might
have been going on with Eddie?

_____

_____

_____

_____

3. How serious was it that Eddie peeked at Tanya's paper? Don't a lot
of people do it occasionally? Explain your answer.

_____

_____

_____

_____

4. How unusual is this kind of cheating in your school?

_____

_____

_____

Cheater!
Cheating

The Story

It seems that every few years there is a major scandal about cheating at a prestigious school. Recently, there was one at the U.S. Naval Academy. Our society has this problem of greatly valuing honesty and self-initiative while acknowledging that our highly competitive society makes those virtues difficult to maintain.

Many young people don't think of the kind of cheating that Eddie did in this little story as stealing, but of course it is. It takes a good deal of maturity for a young person to take steps to make sure that he or she isn't peeking, borrowing, or benefiting from some other student's ideas. Similarly, it takes a little courage to ensure that others aren't taking his or her ideas. This unit is likely to liberate some pent-up feelings on the part of some of your better students, and the discussion could become heated.

The Questions

Eddie undoubtedly had conflicting emotions and values. He probably couldn't live up to his parents' expectations, and so he behaved dishonestly in order to get decent grades. At the same time, it is highly likely that he valued how other students regarded him—but that drive to be liked and admired was losing out to a stronger drive to get at least passing grades. Eddie was undoubtedly someone who needed counseling, and the teacher should have been aware of his predicament.

It's hard to imagine that Eddie didn't care whether his classmates liked him or not. Something else was taking precedence, however, in driving his behavior. Or it might have been that Eddie had different standards than his classmates. He could have possibly come from a school where cheating was a way of life.

If they are honest in responding to the question about peeking at each other's work, your students will admit that at times there is some peeking going on during tests. They might also concede—although it is unlikely—that borrowing homework may be another problem. It happens with math assignments.

We won't try to speculate how your students will respond to the last question about the frequency with which these misdemeanors happen in your school. How they answer will depend a great deal upon the mutual trust you have with them.

An Activity Exploring Cheating

You can administer the activity on page 24, "Uh-oh . . . Better Not," to your students to help them gain additional insights about what has always been a troublesome problem at any school. We know that the more pressure brought to bear on students, the greater the likelihood will be that some cheating will take place. The point of the activity, however, is that there are many different kinds of cheating, all of which go on all of the time.

ACTIVITY

_____   _____
Name   **Date**

Uh-oh . . . Better Not

An activity exploring cheating

There are people who get into
the habit of taking advantage of
situations in which they can do
something most of us think is
wrong. They aren't going to be
arrested for doing these things, and
the chance of their being challenged
when they engage in these acts is usually slim. Nevertheless,
almost everyone considers these behaviors as cheating.

Which of the following actions constitute cheating? Explain why you think
they do or don't.

Is it all right to:

1. claim the tennis ball landed beyond the line when you are sure it didn't?

_____

_____

2. ask your older brother or sister how to do only one problem in your
homework assignment?

_____

_____

3. pretend you are singing with the others in the chorus when you are
really just "mouthing" the words?

_____

_____

Name   Date

4. tell a joke as if you had made it up?

_____

_____

5. take three cookies when you are told you can only have two?

_____

_____

6. stand on your tip-toes when you are being measured for your height?

_____

_____

7. take a "cut" by squeezing in at the front of the line?

_____

_____

8. turn in a book report for a book you haven't read all the way through?

_____

_____

9. wear false eyelashes, hair extensions, or a toupee?

_____

_____

10. tell two different people that you like each of them best?

_____

_____

Open House

Mr. Kelly believed that his class's participation in the school's open house was mainly to show the parents and neighbors what his sixth-grade students were doing. He also believed that his room's participation in the open house was largely the responsibility of his students, and so he wanted a student to coordinate the arrangements and the activities. When he called for a volunteer to be coordinator, a lone hand went up. It was Jay's. No one else wanted to take on the job.

"Oh-oh," thought Mr. Kelly. "This is a big job, and Jay may not be able to handle it." Then he said, "Ah, I see one student has his hand up. Are there any others that would be willing to coordinate our activities?"

Jay's was still the only hand up.

"Well, then . . . Jay has volunteered to be the coordinator," Mr. Kelly said rather slowly. "Let's list on the board what has to be done."

He wrote:

- Contact the newspaper.

- Contact the custodians about seating.

- Contact parents about refreshments.

- Arrange to have the skit videotaped and to have a program printed for it.

- Check with me about work to be displayed.

- Appoint an assistant for each responsibility or activity.

Mr. Kelly thought that the last item on the list would be a safeguard in case Jay needed some help, and he thought it would be likely that he would. Jay's outstanding characteristic was his sincerity. He meant what he said and he always tried to live up to his word. If he promised to do something, he had every intention of doing it. He might not succeed, but it wouldn't be because he didn't try. Jay's sincerity endeared him to his teachers, whereas some of his fellow students weren't nearly so well liked by the staff because they were smart-alecky and not always dependable.

When the open house was only a week away, Mr. Kelly called Jay up to his desk to see how he was coming along with the open house arrangements.

"I couldn't get anyone to help with the refreshments, Mr. Kelly, and so I'm not sure about them yet," Jay explained with a downcast look on his face, "but I will. I did contact *The Daily Gazette*. Trouble is, they haven't phoned me back. I think they'll send someone over. I don't know if there will be a photographer, though. Bill said his dad would bring his camcorder to video the skit. At least, I think he did. There's so much to do, I haven't been able to get it all straight."

Mr. Kelly tried not to frown.

"What about the custodians? They know we'll clean up the room, but we need those extra seats for the audience."

"Oh, I forgot about that. Sorry."

"Did you get some assistants, Jay?" asked Mr. Kelly.

"I tried several kids, but no one was willing to help," replied Jay.

Mr. Kelly was thinking rapidly. Maybe being coordinator was too much for Jay. Mr. Kelly would have to get him some help. Jay wasn't good at enlisting the help of others, but he sure needed some—and soon.

RESPONSES

From *Exploring Character*, Copyright © Good Year Books. This page may be reproduced for classroom use only by the actual purchaser of the book. www.goodyearbooks.com.

Name   **Date**

Open House: Student Responses

Think about your answers to the following questions and write your response to each.

1. Do you think Mr. Kelly will relieve Jay of some of his responsibilities? Why do you think so?

_____

_____

_____

2. What are some reasons for not taking the job of coordinator away from him?

_____

_____

_____

3. Do you think Mr. Kelly should play a bigger role in the preparations himself? Why or why not?

_____

_____

_____

4. Will this experience be good for Jay? Explain.

_____

_____

_____

Open House
Sincerity

The Story

Mr. Kelly had the idea that students should be responsible for their class activities, and so he regularly gave students most of the responsibilities for planning the school's open house. He also believed in asking for volunteers, and that resulted in one of his most sincere, but less able, students becoming coordinator of the open house activities. Jay found that he was probably in over his head as coordinator because he didn't have the requisite organizational skills. When this became apparent, Mr. Kelly faced the dilemma of giving Jay some support or perhaps of relieving him of his responsibilities. Either way, Jay would lose face.

In this story, sincerity counts for a lot, but it doesn't substitute for ability. Nonetheless, we have to have the Jays, who will volunteer and be sincere in their efforts to do right. Jay wasn't a faker or a goof-off; and, if he were, things would have been a lot worse for Mr. Kelly and his class in the forthcoming open house.

The Questions

The first question about Mr. Kelly's relieving Jay of his responsibilities as coordinator will probably be answered in the affirmative by your students. Jay should at least have gotten some help.

A more important consideration is raised by the second question, however, and that centers on Jay's self-concept. The biggest reason for not taking the job away from Jay was that it would have meant a loss of face. Another reason was that it was fairly late in the day to assign a new person to the job. A third reason was that Jay had really been trying to do the job and had succeeded to some extent.

The third question about Mr. Kelly's role in the planning and execution of the open house activities is one that might have occurred to some of your students. Perhaps he should have taken a more active role in the proceedings.

The final question may be interpreted in two ways by your students. Jay could have benefited from being coordinator, especially if he'd never had a chance to take responsibility at school before. (Mr. Kelly believed this was the main reason for having all of his students become leaders in one way or another during the school year.) Some of your students may believe that the experience would be harmful, especially to Jay's ego, because he was probably going to have trouble in the job anyway.

An Activity Exploring Sincerity

The activity following the story will give your students a chance to investigate that elusive trait called sincerity. The dictionary defines *sincere* as "genuine," "true," "honest," and "unfeigned." Generally we think of people as being sincere whose actions match their words or who seem genuine in what they profess to be and do.

The handout on page 30, "But Do They Really Mean It?," poses the question of how we can tell if someone is sincere. One or two of the seven situations are meant to be humorous. Ordinarily, we find out by judging a person's subsequent actions. So, "time will tell." The exercise can be either a group activity or an individual assignment, depending upon the makeup of your class and their sophistication, and you may have to give a little guidance to your students.

ACTIVITY

From *Exploring Character*, Copyright © Good Year Books. This page may be reproduced for classroom use only by the actual purchaser of the book. www.goodyearbooks.com.

Name   **Date**

Have a nice day.

But Do They Really Mean It?

An activity exploring sincerity

There are several ways of declaring one's sincerity, but words are by far the most common way. How can you tell when someone is sincere about his or her feelings or intentions? If we don't see or hear from that individual again, it's hard to tell if the person is being sincere.

Here are some situations in which the question of sincerity might arise. Write your thoughts on the lines below each item.

1.   If a boy says he is going to improve his grades, how can you tell if he is sincere in his intentions?

_____

_____

2.   If a girl says she wants always to be kind to people with disabilities, how can you tell if she means it?

_____

_____

3.   If a saleswoman says to a customer, "That dress is just right for you," how can you tell if she is sincere?

_____

_____

Name _____ **Date** _____

4. If a man says that his greatest concern is for his family, how can we determine how sincere he is?

_____

_____

5. If a man running for Congress says he wants to be elected so he can help "clean up the mess in Washington," how can we tell if he's sincere in what he says?

_____

_____

6. If an old friend tells a man he hasn't seen for 30 years, "You haven't changed a bit," could he be sincere?

_____

_____

7. How should you regard the words of the traffic officer who, after issuing a citation, says: "Have a nice day"?

_____

_____

8. Can you be sincere in stating your intentions but also be quite incapable of doing what you say you'll do? Explain.

_____

_____

_____

_____

_____

The Pageant

Mr. Mitchell and Ms. Nesbitt had a "brainstorm": The school could put on a pageant to portray the important events in the state's history. When they told the other teachers and the principal at a faculty meeting, everyone was quite enthusiastic about the idea. Their students weren't quite as enthusiastic. A few of the girls thought it wasn't a bad idea, but only a couple of the boys wanted to take part in putting on the pageant.

There was a surge of interest, however, when Ms. Nesbitt and Mr. Mitchell buttonholed some of the school's leaders and sold them on the idea. Fairly soon there was a feeling that the pageant would be a first for the school and that it would bring some welcome publicity to Live Oaks Middle School.

Mr. Mitchell had talked to William, Ashley, and Becky about assuming leadership roles in the planning, and Ms. Nesbitt convinced Tom and Ryan that their talents made them the logical choices to take charge of the acting and staging. A number of students showed up at a preliminary meeting in the gym. Among them were Nancy and Curtis.

Nancy was a very good singer and actor. Curtis wasn't known to be especially talented, but he liked to associate himself with the popular members of the student body.

When Tom asked for volunteers to work on props, Curtis raised his hand. He also volunteered to help Ryan with staging the drama, praising Ryan for his musical talents and his past accomplishments as a master of ceremonies.

Before Tom's group had discussed their ideas, he asked Curtis to summarize those ideas on paper and to distribute it at the next session. Curtis made a big show of agreeing to do the task, but then, on the day before the meeting, Tom found that Curtis hadn't written down the ideas. Tom did his best to remember the ideas, and he wrote them up himself.

Curtis didn't do any better for Ryan, who, unfortunately, asked Curtis to dig into all the reference materials he could find and identify songs and dances that were popular during the times depicted by the scenes that were to be presented. Curtis had raised his hand first when Ryan asked who would have time to do the research, but when Ryan checked a week later Curtis hadn't started. He said he was too busy with homework and responsibilities at home to get around to it, but he wanted to continue to "do his part" for Ryan and his group.

RESPONSES

Name   **Date**

The Pageant: Student Responses

Think about your answers to the following questions and write your response to each.

1. Should Ryan and Tom tell Curtis that he needn't bother attending their meetings anymore? Why or why not?

_____

_____

_____

_____

2. Do you think Tom and Ryan realize that Curtis isn't a good person to be assigned an important job? How can you tell when a person isn't really sincere?

_____

_____

_____

3. Do you think Curtis will get another chance to play an important role in either committee? Why or why not?

_____

_____

_____

4. Should Tom consult Mr. Mitchell and Ms. Nesbitt about his committee's problems? Explain.

_____

_____

_____

The Pageant
Insincerity

The Story

It isn't hard to find individuals like Curtis, who try to associate with those they think are popular or powerful so they can feel popular or powerful themselves. They are the sycophants and hangers-on of the world. What would our world be like without them?

The Questions

There is every reason to hope that Ryan and Tom will tell Curtis to "get lost." Both the boys, however, are the kind who don't like to hurt people's feelings.

The outward manifestations of sincerity are an intense or serious look, an intelligent and alert listening posture, and language that is determined, enthusiastic, or quietly forceful. With practice, these outward behaviors are not terribly hard to produce, and they can serve an individual very well in currying favor. The signs of insincerity are harder to discern, but by matching deeds with words, we can often detect an insincere or hypocritical person.

Don't bet that Curtis will give up trying to catch some glory from the pageant. Neither Tom nor Ryan is likely to entrust him with another important task, but chances are that Curtis won't simply bow out of their committees. Individuals like Curtis don't embarrass easily.

The last question brings up the point of whether a teacher should become involved in the problem. Is it better for the students to deal with it all by themselves?

An Activity Exploring Insincerity

Use the activity on page 36, "Do What I Say (Not What I Do)," for investigating one type of sincerity, the common failing of hypocrisy. There are not many people who aren't guilty of being hypocritical at one time or another. However, the hypocrites to worry about are the deliberate ones who do a lot of public posturing about such things as drugs, piety, kindness, honesty, truthfulness, thrift, and gentleness but privately violate those precepts on a regular basis.

The purpose of the exercise is not to make your students more cynical about life but to have them become more aware of the differences between what people say and how they actually behave. Undoubtedly, they have noted hypocrisy in their brief lives and have been confused or dismayed by it. A discussion following the exercise might prove therapeutic.

ACTIVITY

Do What I Say (Not What I Do)

An activity exploring insincerity

Hypocrisy occurs when you say you believe one thing but do the opposite. For example, some people claim to have no racial prejudice, but they won't associate or have dealings with people of certain ethnic groups. Write your thoughts on the lines below.

What is the opposite of:

prejudice? _____

generosity? _____

trust? _____

kindness? _____

fairness? _____

honesty? _____

How do hypocrites behave when they say that they:

hate to argue? _____

dislike sweets? _____

love animals? _____

try to be open-minded? _____

are uncommonly patient? _____

never use bad language? _____

exercise regularly? _____

Do you know any people who are hypocritical about these behaviors? Without naming these people, describe how they act.

_____

_____

_____

The Assignment

The assignment was a tough one, and it was also an important one as far as their grades were concerned. Whether Mr. Mitchell realized it or not, he had made the reference books about Emily Dickinson in the school library the hardest things to find in the school. Mr. Mitchell had read one of Dickinson's riddle poems without giving the first line and then asked his class to identify the poem and relate it to their lives. The purpose of the lesson wasn't just to make a game of finding the poem; it was to emphasize the fact that students can't find all materials using a computer. They couldn't do the assignment without analyzing the riddle poem, and they weren't to share their findings with one another.

There were only three copies of the complete collection of Emily Dickinson's poems in the library, but there were twenty-six copies of various collections of her poems in the library. Becky was absent from school the day that the assignment was made, and so when she returned she was taken by surprise, even though there was another day to do it. Christina was able to check out the last copy of *The Complete Poems of Emily Dickinson*, which was on one-hour reserve. That meant she wouldn't have to return it until 8:00 in the morning. What luck! Leon found out that Christina had managed to get the prized book, and he spread the word that she had an unfair advantage because she had all night to find the poem.

When the class filed into Mr. Mitchell's classroom and handed in their assignments, there were some muttered comments about Christina. It happened that Ryan heard one of them. Because he had been over to see Becky's brother about borrowing a CD the previous night, he knew Christina had taken the book to Becky so that she'd have a chance to find the poem and do the assignment. As class started, he raised his hand.

"Mr. Mitchell, I don't think you know how tough that assignment was. We had two days, but there weren't enough copies of *The Complete Poems of Emily Dickinson* for us to locate the poem without going to a lot of other books."

"Oh, I am sorry, Ryan. I must have been misinformed about the number of copies the library had. By putting it on one-hour reserve, I thought everyone would be able to find the poem."

"But that really made it hard on Becky, who wasn't here on Wednesday," Ryan added.

"Yes, Becky and I talked about that, but she said she'd try to do the assignment on time," said Mr. Mitchell.

"If I'm not mistaken, she was squeezed out. It's lucky there are people like Christina in this class. To get to the library on time, she took off early from her P.E. class. Christina risked getting her grade lowered in P.E. so she could be sure of taking that book home. She wanted Becky to be able to use it last night. Isn't that right, Becky?" Ryan said.

"Yes, it is—and I sure couldn't have found the poem if Christina hadn't brought that book to me last night," Becky replied.

Many of the class turned and looked at Christina, and several smiled at her.

Name   **Date**

The Assignment: Student Responses

Think about your answers to the following questions and write your response to each.

1. Did Ryan get as much credit for being kind to Becky as Christina did? Why or why not?

_____

_____

_____

2. In what other ways could the students have found the poem?

_____

_____

_____

3. What do you think of Mr. Mitchell's assignment?

_____

_____

_____

4. Do you think Mr. Mitchell learned anything from this incident? If so, what?

_____

_____

_____

For the Teacher

The Assignment
Kindness

The Story

There are countless incidents of people being kind to one another every hour of the day. Some of them are performed by young people, and, unfortunately, they mostly go unnoticed. Such was not the case with Becky, Ryan, and Christina in the story. When Christina did a good deed for Becky, it was misinterpreted, and Ryan defended Christina in class. Young people are quick to recognize someone who helps another young person, and so Christina's going to some trouble to help Becky was spontaneously accepted and appreciated by her classmates.

The Questions

Although Christina went out of her way to help Becky and must be given credit for doing a very good deed, Ryan must also be given credit for putting Christina's behavior in the right light. So Ryan was quite kind in defending Christina, while Christina was both resourceful and kind in helping Becky. Ryan, then, was being kind to Christina and not to Becky.

Besides looking in reference books, students could have consulted poetry experts (there are many who specialize in Emily Dickinson's work) or librarians. Mr. Mitchell thought that using the Internet wouldn't work, but he could have been wrong. A great deal of conversation goes on in the Internet, and there might have been some help there from a Dickinson buff. Mr. Mitchell probably selected an obscure riddle poem to make the game more interesting.

Your students will probably scorn Mr. Mitchell's assignment or mildly approve of it, depending upon their academic adventurousness. Undoubtedly they'll identify with his students' frustration in scurrying around and trying to find the right book.

The fourth question concerns Mr. Mitchell's teaching style. It hints that he should at least take more care in making another assignment like this one.

An Activity Exploring Kindness

The activity on page 41, "Happiness Unlimited," will allow your students to further explore the countless ways people are kind to one another.

Name   **Date**

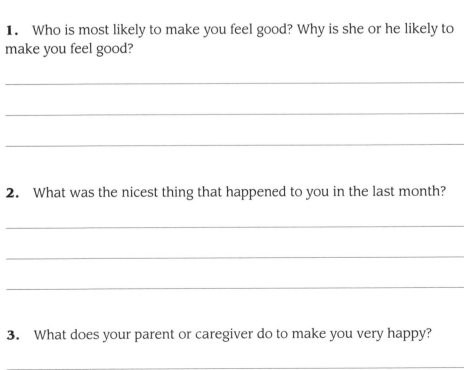

Happiness Unlimited

An activity exploring kindness

There are many, many ways
people have to be nice to one
another. Some give gifts, some
pay compliments, and some go
out of their way to help another person. Here is an opportunity for you
to reflect upon some of the ways you are kind to each other. Write your
thoughts on the lines below.

1. Who is most likely to make you feel good? Why is she or he likely to
make you feel good?

_____

_____

_____

2. What was the nicest thing that happened to you in the last month?

_____

_____

_____

3. What does your parent or caregiver do to make you very happy?

_____

_____

ACTIVITY

_____   _____
Name   Date

4. What can you do to make your parent or caregiver very happy?
Why would it make him or her very happy?

_____

_____

_____

5. What present did you enjoy most during the past year? Why did
you enjoy it so much?

_____

_____

_____

6. What do you do for your best friend that makes him or her happy?

_____

_____

_____

7. What act of kindness makes you feel good every single time
you do it?

_____

_____

_____

The Obstacle Course

Mrs. Bennett had decided what she'd have her sixth-grade class do on Sports Night next Friday night: She would set up two parallel obstacle courses in the gym and divide her class into two teams. In preparation for that night, which would probably draw most of the school's parents, she'd emphasize physical fitness and have students practice in the gym during the week.

Not all of her students were particularly coordinated and the course she set up was a tough one, with tubes to crawl through, a wall to scale, and a rope to swing on over another wall. So there were some spills and skinned knees during practice sessions. A few of the girls and at least one boy found the course very difficult. The one who had the most trouble was Frances, a pleasant but overweight girl who'd been in the class only a month.

Frances was especially nervous about performing in front of a crowd, and she didn't like the idea that the teams would be competing against one another. Frances hadn't made many friends yet, but the members of her team were nice to her when she tried to squeeze through the tube and failed to swing over the wall with the rope in practice. Several encouraged her, but Barry grumbled that their team didn't have a chance with Frances on it.

When Frances told her parents about her fears concerning the obstacle course race, her father said, "I understand that could be bothering you, Hon. Why don't I build a little wall—what's it supposed to be—five feet? I'll make it of sandbags and put it near that big maple in the backyard. Then I'll string up a rope from the limb of the tree so you can practice."

Frances hesitated and then said, "Okay. Thanks, Dad."

But Frances didn't improve very much in her ability to swing over the wall, even though she practiced all week in her yard.

"This is really awful for Frances, Phil," her mother said on Friday morning, about eleven hours from the time Mrs. Bennett's class would be performing at Sports Night.

"Yes, I agree, Doris. All we can do is encourage her," he said gloomily.

The classes made their brief presentations on Friday evening. Mrs. Bennett's class was the last on the program, and that went smoothly—except that Eric, the captain of Frances's team, thought it best to have her go last. If the others got ahead and built up a good lead, maybe Frances wouldn't lose the team's entire lead when she finished the race.

Eric's team was in the lead, and Frances started a good ten seconds before the other team's anchor runner. Disaster struck on the last obstacle, the one where Frances had to swing over the wall on a rope. She hit the wall fairly hard, and, because she was so tense, Frances lost her grip and slowly slipped to the floor. She regained her poise when she reached the floor, and then made a supreme effort and got over the wall. Unfortunately, her counterpart for the other team caught up with her when she slipped to the floor and easily swung over the wall to win the race for her team.

One or two students attempted to comfort a distraught Frances. She put her hands over her face and began sobbing.

Someone said it was tough luck that Frances slipped.

"What did you expect?" Barry stated in a loud voice. "She's too fat to run that course."

_____   _____
Name   **Date**

The Obstacle Course: Student Responses

Think about your answers to the following questions and write your response to each.

1. Was Eric's strategy of having Frances run last a good one?

_____

_____

2. Why couldn't Mrs. Bennett excuse Frances from taking part in the race?

_____

_____

3. When Mrs. Bennett saw the trouble Frances was having, why didn't she simply have the best individuals in the class run the course and not make it a contest between two teams? Did there have to be a competition?

_____

_____

_____

_____

4. Is there any excuse at all for Barry's remark?

_____

_____

For the Teacher

The Obstacle Course
Unkindness

The Story

In spite of the President's Council on Physical Fitness and other national health programs from the past thirty years, our young people become less and less fit every year. Mrs. Bennett was well aware of that fact, and so she wanted to do something to show that her young students could demonstrate a measure of fitness on Sports Night. Unfortunately, Frances and a couple of others weren't ready for the demonstration. The plight of Frances is especially poignant because of her obesity. It is not unusual for pre-pubescent girls to be overweight, but in all likelihood Frances was going to have a problem with her weight for many years to come.

The Questions

It probably wasn't a good idea to have Frances run last because it put more pressure on her.

Mrs. Bennett divided her class into two teams, so if Frances had been excused (and that might have been embarrassing for her), one of the other students couldn't participate. It was an awkward situation for Mrs. Bennett.

Mrs. Bennett could have changed the performance so that there was no race. Her class didn't have to stage a competition, but it was her idea that it would be more exciting for the students and for the audience. It did turn out to be an exciting race, but a price was paid.

There is no excuse for a cruel remark such as Barry's. He was disappointed that his team lost, but that's no justification for what he said.

An Activity Exploring Unkindness

"Words That Hurt," on page 47, shines a spotlight on the most common kind of unkindness—name-calling. You may well question our idea of listing offensive words and names because it is possible that many of your students will be learning about them for the first time. On the other hand, many a youngster (and adult) has used an epithet in ignorance and innocence, thinking it was harmless.

This exercise is probably most effective when administered to the class as a whole. Give your students a chance to read it silently first. Then write the adjectives shown, such as *overweight* and *thin* on the chalkboard. Last, list the words that the class offers.

This exercise sticks to personal kinds of verbal put-downs. It is wise to stay away from ethnic slurs in this exercise. There may be other opportunities for dealing with those hurtful words.

ACTIVITY

Name

Date

Words That Hurt

An activity exploring unkindness

Sometimes people aren't aware that the ways in which they talk about other people can really bother them. There are quite a large number of names that young people call each other that are meant to be insulting, but there are others that aren't designed to hurt. These can still hurt feelings, though. For example, people who don't want to describe a certain girl as "skinny" say that she is "painfully thin." That expression might hurt just as much.

You can become more sensitive to words with which you may unintentionally hurt others. A good start would be to write down those words that disturb you and your friends. Here are some common adjectives that accurately describe a trait or condition. What hurtful words are sometimes used instead?

overweight _____

thin _____

slow (in schoolwork) _____

bright (in schoolwork) _____

short _____

very tall _____

awkward _____

unstylish _____

bad-complexioned _____

redheaded _____

immature _____

Anna

It was hard for Mr. Naylor not to be impressed with Anna. She had been a newcomer to Irving School, but right away she fit in with her classmates beautifully. The kids accepted her for being the unaffected and sweet person she was. You'd never know that Anna was probably a young genius, thought Mr. Naylor. She hadn't missed a question when she took the mental maturity test in the fall.

Her classmates realized that Anna excelled in all of her studies, but they weren't envious of her in the least. Although enthusiastic about all of the subjects Mr. Naylor taught, Anna was modest about her accomplishments. She wrote and directed a Halloween play but was never bossy in doing so.

Life hadn't been all peaches and cream for Anna, however. Her parents had divorced a few years before she entered Mr. Naylor's class. She didn't see her father much, but her mother, a small shop owner, was doing a good job of raising Anna. In addition, Anna had a physical challenge: Because of an illness when she was a young child, Anna's left foot splayed a bit and she wasn't nimble. Regardless, Anna was an eager, if not proficient, participant in all of the playground games.

In the spring Mr. Naylor learned that the local American Legion post was cooperating with other posts nearby in sponsoring a county-wide essay contest. The topic was "Why the United States is a great country." Mr. Naylor told his class that if any of his students wanted to enter the contest, he would submit their essays to the American Legion post. Three girls and a boy wrote essays on their own time, and one was Anna. Mr. Naylor didn't give much more thought to the contest until he was called to the principal's office a month later. Mr. Crosby told him that a call had come in from a reporter who worked for the local weekly newspaper. The reporter had phoned to inform Mr. Crosby that Anna had won first prize in the contest.

When Mr. Naylor told the class, there was wild cheering in the classroom. Anna blushed a little. The event was commemorated by headlines in the class newspaper ("Anna Wins!"), and a photographer came with the reporter to take Anna's picture, along with an official from the local American Legion post and Mr. Naylor. She was presented with a check for $100 and a certificate.

As the school day came to a close on the following day, Anna asked Mr. Naylor if she could do something before class was dismissed. He agreed. Then, with a very, very brief explanation, Anna passed out equal amounts of her $100 award to every member of the class. They were delighted, but Mr. Naylor was flabbergasted. Even for Anna, it was quite a gesture.

_____   _____
Name   **Date**

Anna: Student Responses

Think about your answers to the following questions and write your response to each.

1. Why did Anna divide the money among her classmates?

_____

_____

_____

2. Would you have thought to share your prize money with your classmates?

_____

_____

3. Who do you think Anna asked to appear in the newspaper photo with her? Why?

_____

_____

_____

4. The class was delighted with Anna's winning the prize and displayed no jealousy. Is this unusual? Explain.

_____

_____

_____

Anna
Generosity

The Story

Incredible as it may seem, nearly every detail of this story is true. On the other hand, you may be one of those lucky people who believe that there is a lot more goodness in children than they get credit for. Anna was special, but then so was Mr. Naylor's class as a whole. Fortunately for Anna, there were several other bright students in the class, and so she didn't seem so unusual in her achievements.

The Questions

There could be students in your class who are inclined to believe that Anna was buying some popularity when she divided her $100 prize among her classmates. It's been known to happen—with candy, gum, presents, parties, and even money. However, at the beginning of the story, students are told that Anna is already popular. A cynical person could imagine that she was trying to become more popular or had some motive for being generous. Anna had no such notions in her mind or heart.

We recognize that the question of whether a student would do as Anna did is foolish in some ways. It will be difficult for a student to claim that he or she would probably have given away the prize money, as Anna did. Nevertheless, we wanted to ask that very question because that is one of the thoughts that will occur to your students, namely, "Would I ever do something like that?"

The inference in the last question is that Anna insisted that her teacher appear in the photo to appear in the local paper. It was typical of her to want to share the glory.

The matter of jealousy isn't raised in the story, and your students may have a nagging question about that. Were *all* of her classmates sincerely happy for Anna when she won the essay contest?

An Activity Exploring Generosity

Engage your students in a little practical research after they have answered the questions about Anna. First, discuss what constitutes a generous act by asking them to describe acts of generosity. Then have your students spend two days (or longer if you wish) in identifying generous acts performed in the classroom, on the playground, in the neighborhood, and at home. Before starting, ask students to guess where they will observe the most incidents. Then have them keep a journal in which they jot down the acts as they see or hear them. At the end of the two days, hold a class discussion on their findings.

Kerry

Kerry was a twelve-year-old with a lot of enthusiasm. He collected baseball cards, had an aquarium of tropical fish in his room, and was crazy about computer games. He had been in the top third of his sixth-grade class and had been a sure bet to volunteer for any project his teacher suggested.

Because Kerry had a very generous allowance, he was able to get more baseball cards than anyone else in the school. In fact, whenever Kerry heard of someone having a card he didn't have, he wasn't happy until he'd traded for it or bought it. As far as his computer game collection was concerned, probably no one in town had a better one.

During the summer after sixth grade, Kerry noticed that the yellow apples had ripened on a tree in his backyard. The tree was loaded with apples—a bumper crop! Kerry knew his father would give him some money if he would pick a basketful of the apples. His father had warned him to be careful when picking the apples, however, because the tree limbs were heavy with fruit and sagged.

Kerry was able to pick a basketful of apples quickly, but to pick a second basketful he'd have to go out on the main branches and lean on them. He really had enough apples, and there was no hurry. Kerry's dad would be pleased with a whole basket of apples. Nevertheless, he thought he would sell a second basketful to his neighbor, Mr. Norris. The extra money would enable him to buy that computer game he'd been wanting.

As he edged out on the biggest limb, Kerry managed to get quite a few apples. Then he crawled out on a smaller limb. C-r-r-a-a-c-k! Kerry crashed to the ground. No bones were broken, and he thought only his pride was hurt, but then Kerry realized that he had fallen on the first basket of apples and had squashed most of them!

RESPONSES

Name   Date

Kerry: Student Responses

Think about your answers to the following questions and write your response to each.

1. Do you admire Kerry for being enterprising and trying to pick another basketful of apples? Why or why not?

_____

_____

_____

2. Do you know anyone like Kerry? Without naming the person, tell how he or she is like Kerry.

_____

_____

_____

3. Which of Aesop's fables reminds you most of this story about Kerry?

_____

_____

4. Because a limb of the apple tree was broken, do you think Kerry got into trouble (especially after his father had warned him)?

_____

_____

_____

For the Teacher ———

Kerry
Greed

The Story

This tale is supposed to point up a common problem among children who don't know when "enough is enough." Kerry has energy, but he also a large dose of acquisitiveness. The story may or may not bring forth some memories in your students. Most youngsters have climbed trees, and not a few have broken branches and fallen.

The Questions

Because Kerry was foolish not to use a ladder and also to climb out on a limb that was already sagging, your students will probably not give him credit for being enterprising.

Students should answer the second question privately because of the possibility of hurting someone's feelings. We ask it simply to help make the story more relevant to the lives of your students.

The story is frankly based on the Aesop fable about the fox and the grapes. It will be interesting for you to learn how many of your students are familiar with those fables.

We'll guess that some of your students will think that Kerry is a spoiled brat, and so they'll doubt if he was punished by his father. Should he be?

An Activity Exploring Greed

The exercise "Too Much" on page 56 is designed to encourage your students to think more deeply about the concept of greed. Almost without exception, greediness is considered a bad characteristic. As a warm-up to this exercise, ask your students if they can think of an exception.

_____   _____
Name   **Date**

Too Much

An activity exploring greed

Greed is the word we use to
name a strong desire to acquire
more than is needed, whether
it is money, possessions, food,
attention, praise, power, or
land. The way to distinguish
greed from ambition is to determine whether an individual's desires are
excessive. Write your answers to the following questions.

1. Is it possible to be greedy with regard to winning competitions and
acquiring trophies? Explain.

_____

_____

_____

2. Is it possible to be greedy in having new experiences, such as
traveling to new places and engaging in new activities? Explain.

_____

_____

_____

3. Is it possible to be greedy in acquiring knowledge? If so, what is the
harm in being greedy about knowledge—are scholars greedy?

_____

_____

_____

Name   Date

4. Is it possible to be greedy about having friends? If you think so, what is the matter with having too many friends?

_____

_____

_____

5. Is it possible to be greedy about looking for thrills? Explain.

_____

_____

_____

6. Is it possible to be greedy when it comes to helping others? Why do you think so?

_____

_____

_____

7. The United States consumes, per person, far more of the world's production of oil than any other country. Are the people of the United States being greedy in doing so? Why or why not?

_____

_____

Do you feel guilty about the consumption of oil by your country? Explain.

_____

_____

Rhonda

It was unusual for Rhonda to share a pack of gum with anyone, but she offered Sue a stick today. Sue wasn't much of a gum chewer. She had gotten the idea at home that there was something a little gross about chewing gum, especially when a person was making a display of it or making smacking noises. But Sue was also taught to be polite, and she accepted the stick of gum. Uncharacteristically, Rhonda asked her if she'd like another stick for later, but Sue politely declined the offer.

Everyone knew Rhonda's father was manager of the chewing gum plant on the north side of town, and nearly everyone had been disappointed because Rhonda very rarely gave away any of the gum that her father gave to her. Mrs. Thomas, Rhonda's mother, had mentioned to several mothers that Mr. Thomas regularly gave Rhonda a good deal of the gum the factory had for promotional purposes and that she was glad that their daughters could have the gum, if they were fond of it. Instead of giving it away, Rhonda was hoarding that gum in her closet.

The reason Rhonda was offering gum to Sue was that she thought Sue would share one of the two cupcakes she always brought for lunch. It was morning recess, so Rhonda thought that she would manage to sit next to Sue at lunch, and Sue might be generous with a cupcake. Rhonda had seen her share cupcakes before.

Tina happened to be a great gum chewer, and she had heard that they were trying out a new flavor at the factory. At lunch she felt bold enough to ask Rhonda about the raspberry-flavored gum she'd heard about from a girl whose father works at the factory. When she had asked Rhonda about the raspberry-flavored gum, Rhonda said she would have to ask her father about it. Maybe it wasn't available yet. Tina's friend had told her that the gum was wonderful, and so she just gave Rhonda a knowing smile and said she'd like to try the gum when it was available. Rhonda said she didn't know when that would happen and changed the subject.

RESPONSES

_____   _____
Name   **Date**

Rhonda: Student Responses

Think about your answers to the following questions and write your response to each.

1. Obviously Rhonda knew all about the raspberry-flavored gum. Was she just being selfish by being evasive about it? Explain.

_____

_____

_____

2. What could happen if Rhonda's father discovers that Rhonda is hoarding the gum he gives to her?

_____

_____

_____

3. Why do think people hoard things?

_____

_____

_____

4. Give another example of someone offering a gift in order to get something in return.

_____

_____

_____

Rhonda
Stinginess

The Story

Children are taught to share, but in their first years it doesn't come naturally to them. By the time they enter school, most are aware that they should share their toys and other possessions with their peers, even if they don't want to. Rhonda didn't quite get over the early childhood stage of being egocentric and selfish. If she persists in her selfishness, Rhonda will have some very tough times as an adolescent and as an adult.

The Questions

Tina was quite sure Rhonda had chewed some of the new raspberry-flavored gum and that Rhonda was simply being evasive about it because she didn't intend to share any of it. In a way, Tina was needling Rhonda.

Without knowing anything about his personality, it's hard to guess what Rhonda's father might do if he discovers that Rhonda is not giving away most of the gum. Perhaps he wants her to do so, probably because it is part of his idea of promoting the gum and partly because he imagines it makes her a little more popular.

Hoarding is a form of selfishness. When it isn't part of a plan, the reasons for hoarding are psychological. The person who hoards thinks that a commodity is in short supply or might become scarce some time in the future. It's the "I've got mine" thinking that also implies "I'm not concerned whether you have yours or not."

The fourth question brings up the universal ploy of giving something to get something in return—the basis of bribery and social exchanges alike. This may be the most interesting of the issues brought up in this unit.

An Activity Exploring Stinginess

The final question following the story—asking for examples of someone giving a gift in order to get something in exchange—offers an opportunity for some role-playing. After your students respond to the question, select one response and have volunteers act out the parts. It will be revealing to see this ploy acted out.

Matt's Regimen

That's about all there is to it, Matt," Mr. Murray said. "You just have to water for an hour and a half every other day and make sure the temperature is around 80° in the greenhouse. Oh yes, make sure the mister is operating. It has to be humid in there."

"No problem, Dad. I can remember those few things," Matt said cheerfully.

"Yes, I'm sure you can," his father replied.

"Oh, Matt!" called out Gloria. "Don't forget that my rabbits need water every day, too!"

"Okay, Gloria. I won't forget," promised Matt.

Gloria, who was sixteen, was off to summer camp as a counselor, leaving at almost the same time as her parents, who were going to the coast for two weeks. That left Matt and his twenty-year-old sister Lena to "guard the fort," along with the family's dog, Beans. Lena wouldn't be around much, though, because she worked at a fast-food restaurant during the week and went out with Phil during the weekends. She was supposed to keep an eye on Matt, cook his dinner, and make sure he didn't stay up too late. Matt liked to watch television in the evening, but he usually went to bed at 10:30 or so.

Matt performed his chores without forgetting anything for the first two days. Because it was hot, he went swimming with Ryan at the community pool before returning home to water the lawn and garden at 4:30. On the third day, Gloria phoned from camp and wanted to know if her rabbits were getting water and food.

"No, I haven't forgotten your rabbits, Gloria," Matt responded to her nervous query. "They're doing fine. Even Beans hasn't paid any attention to them lately."

For his birthday Matt had received a waterproof wristwatch with several functions, one of which was an alarm that he set every morning in order to be sure to remember his chores. It served him well two days later when he lost track of time at the pool and was reminded by his watch that he had to head home to do the afternoon watering.

"Why doesn't Dad have a timer on his hoses like Ryan's father has?" thought Matt as he hurried home. "It would sure make watering easier."

During dinner, after a week had gone by, Lena asked Matt, "Have you forgotten to do anything yet, Matt?"

"Naw. There's not a lot to do. It's no big deal," replied Matt.

At the end of the two weeks, Mr. and Mrs. Murray pulled into the garage just before dinner time. Matt greeted them with a grin.

"How'd it go, Matt?" Mr. Murray asked.

"Fine, Dad. Just fine. I didn't miss a day at the pool. It was over 90° every day," responded Matt.

"Good. I see the lawns and shrubs look okay in spite of the heat. Let's take at look at the greenhouse."

Matt accompanied his father to the greenhouse and Beans tagged along. "Great! My orchids look fine. You did a good job, Matt!"

"Thanks, Dad," Matt said with a shy smile.

RESPONSES

From *Exploring Character*, Copyright © Good Year Books. This page may be reproduced for classroom use only by the actual purchaser of the book. www.goodyearbooks.com.

Name   Date

Matt's Regimen: Student Responses

Think about your answers to the following questions and write your response to each.

1. Why do you think Mr. Murray had more confidence in Matt's remembering to do his chores than his sister Gloria did?

_____

_____

_____

2. Is it unusual for an eighth grader such as Matt to be trustworthy? Why do you think so?

_____

_____

_____

3. The chores didn't seem to spoil Matt's fun. Who do you think did the dishes and cleaned the house? Why do you think so?

_____

_____

_____

4. Do you think Gloria revised her opinion of Matt's trustworthiness? Explain.

_____

_____

_____

Matt's Regimen
Reliability

The Story

This story is meant to be about a parent's trust in his son. Matt was entrusted with the care of his sister's rabbits when she goes to summer camp, but his main chores were to water the lawns and maintain the greenhouse for his father. Matt's sister Lena was with him at home, but mostly he was on his own. Matt still managed to have some fun by going swimming every day. He was nonchalant about carrying out his duties, and, to everyone's surprise but his father's, he did a very good job. This scenario is played out every summer by boys and girls in much the same way.

The Questions

Perhaps the fact that his father had confidence in Matt and gave him responsibility for the garden and greenhouse bolstered Matt and made it easy to fulfill Mr. Murray's expectations. Another explanation for Matt's coming through was that he was trustworthy.

Eighth-grade boys are famous for being unpredictable and not terribly reliable—but those may just be the impressions of older generations. How your students perceive themselves and all fourteen-year-olds will be fascinating.

Probably the dishes were shared by Matt and his sister, but he also may have done some of the housekeeping because Lena was busy with work and dating. As you know, it isn't unusual for boys to do household chores, too.

Regarding Gloria's opinion of Matt's trustworthiness, one or more students might think that her opinion won't change permanently until he has demonstrated, a few more times, that he is dependable.

An Activity Exploring Reliability

You might try to sharpen your students' ideas about that important virtue, reliability, by asking them to interpret these three oxymorons:

- Erratic reliability
- Dependable goof-off
- Trusty traitor

Present the oxymorons, one at a time, and encourage as many interpretations as possible.

Harry's Job

Thirteen-year-old Harry had a job. Every weekday, he had to take care of his four-year-old brother Danny after school. Harry had been doing this for almost two years, ever since his parents' divorce.

Harry's mother worked at a nearby theater selling tickets. Her shift started at 1 p.m. and ended at 9 p.m. Monday through Friday. She usually drove Danny and Mrs. Gibbons's daughter Alyssa to a day care center on her way to work. Mrs. Gibbons brought Danny home every day, and Harry usually got home just minutes before Danny arrived.

There were times when it was very hard for Harry to turn down an invitation from his friends to play basketball after school or to look for crawdads at the creek, but only once was he ever late getting home—and that was only for fifteen minutes. He and Tim had been tussling in the back of the room during class, and Ms. Nesbitt made them stay after school, cleaning up the room. Mrs. Gibbons was waiting patiently with Danny at the front door when Harry arrived home. She wasn't upset because Harry was almost never late, so she knew he probably had a good reason for being late that day.

Every day just before 6 p.m., Harry warmed up whatever dinner his mother had left. Once or twice he had burned a casserole, but he almost always was able to serve his brother a good meal.

There was a scary time one evening in January when two older boys were fighting outside the apartment, and one had a knife. Harry and Danny stayed inside, but they could see some of the commotion, and Harry knew one of the boys. When the boy with the knife stabbed his adversary in the shoulder and Harry saw blood on his shirt, he phoned 9-1-1. The police and paramedics came in a few minutes and gave the wounded boy first aid. The boy with the knife had fled when he heard the police siren. When Harry's mother came home that night and heard about the fight, she told Harry that he had done the right thing. She shivered a little, and then thought to herself how fortunate she was to have a son like Harry.

RESPONSES

Harry's Job: Student Responses

Think about your answers to the following questions and write your response to each.

1. Is Harry different from most boys his age? If so, how?

_____

_____

_____

2. What is Harry losing by devoting his afternoons and evenings to caring for his little brother?

_____

_____

_____

3. What is he gaining?

_____

_____

_____

4. Harry and Danny are sometimes called "latchkey kids." They usually go home to an apartment or house where no adult is present. Does that kind of situation help young people become more responsible? Why or why not?

_____

_____

_____

Harry's Job
Dependability

The Story

One might think that Harry is saddled with too much child care for a young person of thirteen. His situation isn't terribly different from that of a great many other older siblings. After his parents divorced, his father began paying child support but not alimony, and Harry's mother, who hadn't worked outside her home for awhile, had to seek employment. She doesn't make enough money at the theater to pay for a baby-sitter in the afternoon and evening, and so she has Harry take care of Danny until she comes home after 9:00.

The Questions

The point of asking whether Harry is different from most thirteen-year-olds is that he is and he isn't. Unfortunately, many young people these days have responsibilities identical or similar to Harry's because often there is no one at home when children come home from school. Whether he is more conscientious than the typical young person in his position is for your students to decide, based upon their own experiences and knowledge.

Obviously, Harry is being deprived of time with his peers in the afternoons and evenings, a time highly valued by most youngsters. However, Harry knows that he is making a contribution to his family's welfare. He is becoming more mature by giving up his time and sacrificing his own desires in order to help his mother and little brother.

Depending on students' own situations at home, they may have strong views concerning supervision. Whether or not responsibility such as Harry's will make him more responsible as he grows up becomes a matter of how he handles his job. This ultimately depends on the young person.

An Activity Exploring Dependability

Thinking of our responsibilities is seldom an exhilarating experience. Nevertheless, the activity on page 70 is one that can be enlightening for your students. Everyone has responsibilities, and others depend on us to be responsible. Some of us take this more seriously than do others, but those that shirk responsibility pay a price. We hope your students will grasp this fact of life.

ACTIVITY

Responsibilities

An activity exploring dependability

All of us have responsibilities to other people—not the least of which is that we all be civil to one another. We have other responsibilities, too—to pets, to institutions such as our city, and to friends. We are supposed to be responsible for our actions also. If we don't take responsibility for our actions, we will soon be in trouble with others and, perhaps, the law. What are your responsibilities for each of these parts of your life? Try to name at least two ways in which you are personally responsible.

1. Your family members:

_____

_____

_____

2. Your appearance:

_____

_____

_____

ACTIVITY

_____   _____
            Name   **Date**

3. Your behavior in games:

_____

_____

_____

4. Your behavior in class:

_____

_____

_____

5. Your behavior in an argument:

_____

_____

_____

6. Your behavior in a social gathering:

_____

_____

_____

7. Your behavior in an emergency such as a fire or an accident:

_____

_____

_____

Nina on First?

I sure hope she shows up. It's almost time to start practice," Becky grumbled to Christina.

"Yeah, it would be just like Trisha not to come. Didn't she miss practice last week?" Christina responded.

"And that wasn't the only time she didn't show up—but this practice is important. The game with Orono is on Saturday. They're *tough!* Trisha may be a flake, but she can hit," said Becky.

"Uh-huh, and if Trisha can't play on Saturday, Nina will be at first base," moaned Christina.

"Mmmm. You're right, Christina. Nina hasn't had a hit in a long time," returned Becky.

A few minutes later Ms. Townsend, the popular coach of Live Oaks' softball team, started practice with some drills—without Trisha. When they had batting practice, Nina tried hard but wasn't able to hit the ball out of the infield. "It doesn't matter that Nina can't hit," Ms. Townsend said to herself. "She tries, and that's what is important."

The next day at school Christina and Becky encountered Trisha in the hallway. "Missed you at practice yesterday, Trisha," Becky said in a somewhat disgruntled voice.

"Oh, that. I couldn't make it. My cousin wanted me to come over to her house after school and meet some guys. We had a lot of fun eating sundaes and playing video games," Trisha explained in a matter-of-fact way.

"Well, I sure hope you can find time in your busy schedule to make it to the game Saturday," Christina said sarcastically.

Name   Date

Nina on First?: Student Responses

Think about your answers to the following questions and write your response to each.

1. Do you think Trisha will show up for the game with Orono on Saturday? Why or why not?

_____

_____

_____

2. Should Ms. Townsend allow Trisha to play in the game? Explain your reasoning.

_____

_____

_____

_____

3. Should Ms. Townsend start Nina at first base, regardless of whether Trisha shows up for the game? Explain why or why not.

_____

_____

_____

_____

4. What do you think is wrong with this situation, in which the coach doesn't know whether Trisha will show up for the game?

_____

_____

_____

Nina on First?
Unreliability

The Story

Young athletes—both girls and boys—often get spoiled these days, and if they are talented the pampering comes early in their careers. Trisha may or may not be a gifted athlete, but she already seems to believe that she is special. If she reaches the stage where she thinks rules are for everybody else (and we do have a great number of athletes in this country who think that way), Trisha will be in trouble. Once a young person perceives herself or himself to be necessary to a team's success, it is easy to get an exaggerated sense of her or his own importance. Our society certainly makes successful athletes feel privileged.

The Questions

Our guess is that Trisha did show up for the game. It probably was a chance for her to get some attention and perhaps some accolades. Your students will probably think so also.

Ms. Townsend's role as coach and role model is not dealt with in the story, but she obviously can play an important part in resolving the problem of Trisha's unreliable ways. Judging from Ms. Townsend's comment to herself about Nina, winning isn't everything to her. Ms. Townsend might be tempted to tell Trisha that she is needed and should be at the game on Saturday, but she will probably not do so.

Many of your students would probably start Nina, if only to spite Trisha. There are many coaches at all levels of athletics who bench a player for violating rules or misbehavior—but only for the start of the game. Then they send the player into the game. Usually winning is too important to them to suspend the player, but that does happen sometimes in high school and college athletics.

The situation is wrong because rules are rules, for all team members, including Trisha. Discipline breaks down whenever one individual is allowed to break the rules without consequences. In addition, in all team sports, practice is important. If Trisha doesn't work out with the team, she's letting them, and herself, down.

An Activity Exploring Unreliability

Most of your students are probably involved in either team or individual sports. Hold a class discussion, asking students if they've ever missed a practice or game. What happened after they missed practice? Did their coach or teacher treat them any differently afterward? Have other team members missed a practice or game? Did those team members experience the same consequences as your students? Last, have students talk about their attitudes concerning missed practices or missed games. How did they feel about their playing the next time they were with their team or in their class?

Toby's Bike

Toby looked at his shoes. They were a little scuffed up, but they would be all right to wear to the party. Besides, no one paid any attention to shoes at Darrell's parties. Unfortunately, it was a birthday party, and he hadn't gotten a present for Darrell. Well, there was still time to go to Long's Pharmacy. Or was there? He was supposed to be at the party in a half-hour. Maybe he could find something in his room and wrap it up with some of the fancy wrapping paper his mother kept in the den. That would be better than rushing to Long's and trying to find a gift.

What about one of those crazy presents he'd gotten for Christmas and had never used? He would never use them, anyway. A pen set—Toby hated to write anything, most of all letters. A book about ancient

Rome—ugh! A red-and-blue tie—Darrell wouldn't be any happier to get that than he was! A wristwatch with an alarm—well, he didn't like to be reminded when he was late. Yeah, maybe Darrell would like that watch.

Uh-oh. Only twenty-five minutes before he was supposed to be at Darrell's. And Darrell's house was across town—twenty minutes away on his bike. His bike? N-o-o-o!! Toby's bike had a flat tire! It had been flat for a week. Every day he told himself that he wasn't going to be riding it, so why bother patching it or getting a new tire? No hurry. The only one who could drive him to the party was his older sister, and she had told Toby last time that she wouldn't drive him again. What a lousy sister!

Nuts! Toby really wanted to go to the party. He hadn't paid any attention when his mother reminded him an hour ago to get ready for it as she and his father left for the movie. Well, there wasn't anything to do now but to ask his sister to drive him there . . . and to wrap that crummy present. Why did he have all the bad luck?

From *Exploring Character*, Copyright © Good Year Books. This page may be reproduced for classroom use only by the actual purchaser of the book. www.goodyearbooks.com.

Name _____ **Date** _____

Toby's Bike: Student Responses

Think about your answers to the following questions and write your response to each.

1. What do you think Toby was doing when he realized the party was only a half-hour away?

_____

_____

_____

2. Do you think Toby got to the party on time? Why or why not?

_____

_____

_____

3. Do you know anyone like Toby? Without naming names, tell why he or she is like Toby.

_____

_____

_____

4. What do you think about Toby giving his watch as a birthday present to Darrell?

_____

_____

_____

5. What name do we give to behavior like Toby's?

_____

For the Teacher

Toby's Bike
Procrastination

The Story

Toby isn't an extreme example of a procrastinator. He's rather typical. People like Toby go through life in a rush because they don't plan well and because they are always acting as if there is plenty of time when there isn't enough. In truth, they are gamblers and optimists. (We suppose all gamblers must be optimists—or masochists.) They continually put things off, believing that it will be all right in the end; something or somebody will come through for them. Procrastinators are especially hard to reform. Their ways become entrenched, and they don't seem to learn from their experiences.

The Questions

Your students will probably think that Toby was fooling around—doing nothing important—when he realized that the party was to start in a half-hour. Procrastinators dawdle.

The chances are good that Toby was late. He would have had to spend some precious moments convincing his sister to drive him to the party. Otherwise, he had to walk. Even if he could have caught a bus right away, he'd be twenty or thirty minutes late.

Hopefully those of your students who are like Toby will recognize themselves in him. If they are borderline procrastinators, they may possibly see that their ways should be mended.

The idea of giving someone a gift you don't like will—or should—bother some of your students. We're not trying to suggest that it is a good solution to Toby's problem about finding a birthday present, but perhaps Darrell appreciated the watch a good deal more than Toby has. If Toby's father learns of the act, however, he might be quite upset.

The word *procrastination* doesn't appear in the story, but it's a handy word to know for naming behavior that is all too common.

An Activity Exploring Procrastination

Your students are just old enough to have had an experience or two with that awful feeling that "it's too late," as when a grandmother has died and it is too late to thank her or to say they loved her. When they were a little younger, the finality of death didn't sink in, and they didn't feel the loss, guilt, and helplessness so much. With their increasing maturity, your students should recognize the poignancy of such a situation.

The activity is about procrastination. It raises the often painful question of "What can be done now?" In some cases it is best to do nothing, but there are times when an appropriate action is called for afterward. Most of the situations presented in the exercise can be remedied in part by an action by the procrastinator.

Name

Date

When It's Too Late

An activity exploring procrastination

There are times when we are unhappy with ourselves because we didn't get around to doing something we should have done. For example, you might have really wanted to enter a contest but you kept putting off filling in the entry blank and mailing it in. Once the deadline passed, there was no way to become eligible for the prize—you'd blown it! That's the way it is with a great many opportunities in life. Following are seven occasions for remorse, frustration, and guilt when someone puts off something that should have been done. Write your thoughts on the lines below each question.

What can you do, if anything, when:

1. the bus has departed and you missed it?

_____

_____

_____

2. you have put a letter in the mailbox at the post office and then realized you'd forgotten to put in your most important news?

_____

_____

_____

ACTIVITY

3. the deadline has passed for turning in an important application?

_____

_____

_____

4. you have said something in anger to a friend?

_____

_____

_____

5. you have had your hair cut very short and you look awful?

_____

_____

_____

6. the race is over and you arrived too late to run in it?

_____

_____

_____

7. a loved one died and you weren't able to say goodbye?

_____

_____

_____

The Play

Ms. Benson had given a good deal of thought to the idea of putting on a play for the parents before she took the plunge and asked her students if they would like to do it. They were enthusiastic about performing a play, as she knew they would be, but Ms. Benson had a few misgivings. For one thing, it would take time away from regular lessons, and this class wasn't so advanced that they could afford to put off their lessons in math, language arts, and social studies. Ms. Benson knew that she didn't have a lot of experience directing plays, either, which made her a little uneasy.

Ms. Benson decided to hold try-outs for the two largest roles and then assign all of the other parts. In the auditions it was apparent that Nancy and Bill were the best choices for the leading parts. She then assigned the other twenty-two parts to her other students. Her only worry was the role she gave Jess, who stuttered badly, especially when he was stressed. Ms. Benson decided to give Jess a small part with two lines. He had been having daily sessions with the school speech therapist and was making progress. Nevertheless, Ms. Benson and his parents were worried.

"Jess, are you sure you want to be in that play?" his mother asked him. "You're coming along fine in those sessions with Mr. Brodsky, but maybe you should wait for a while before you act in a play before a lot of people."

"—no, Mom. I want t-t-to do it," Jess said. "Every kid has to have a part. I d-d-don't want to be the only one who isn't in the p-p-play."

Jess's mom gave him a hug and said, "I know you'll do just fine, honey."

During the rehearsals the students, including Jess, spoke their lines confidently. They were a wonderful group, Ms. Benson thought. She was still worried about how Jess would deliver his lines, however; he was able to go through both rehearsals without stuttering or stammering, but how would he do before an audience of adults?

Jess was also concerned. He'd always been excused from saying anything in plays in the lower grades. Although he understood why he was left out, he had been hurt. Jess knew that he was putting himself on the spot. Everyone—students *and* parents—knew he had a speech problem. It would be scary, all right. "Never mind," he told himself. "I'll show them!"

On the night of the play there were a few mishaps, but everything went well. When it was time for Jess to speak, Ms. Benson and his parents held their breath. Except for hesitating a little before the second line, Jess was perfect. Many individuals in the classroom smiled to themselves when Jess had finished. He had come through.

As Ms. Benson remarked after the play to the principal, "That's one brave boy!"

Name

Date

The Play: Student Responses

Think about your answers to the following questions and write your response to each.

1. What would have been the consequences if Jess hadn't been able to say his lines?

_____

_____

_____

2. Many people are afraid of speaking in front of an audience, even if they know everyone in it. Are you very uneasy speaking to a group? How can someone overcome the fear of speaking before an audience?

_____

_____

_____

3. Would Ms. Benson have been justified in refusing to let Jess be in the play, even though he wanted to be? Explain.

_____

_____

_____

4. Ms. Benson was taking a chance by letting Jess insist on being in the play. Was she also being brave? Why or why not?

_____

_____

_____

The Play
Bravery

The Story

There are a great many ways in which a person can be brave. In all cases, the individual overcomes a fear. In the case of Jess, it was a matter of overcoming a fear of embarrassment and also of letting himself and others down. Stuttering is unfortunately a common problem among young people, and its origins and remedies are still largely mysterious. Basketball great Bill Walton had a stuttering problem that he overcame to the extent that he became a prominent television sports broadcaster.

The Questions

The first question could lead your students into thinking more deeply about the forces that come into play when students perform for audiences. Jess's progress in overcoming his speech disorder could have been stopped if he had failed to deliver his lines. The individual who has problems speaking properly is usually suffering from an emotional disturbance. He or she must gain confidence that the problem can be overcome. His classmates would have been kind and not mentioned his muffing his lines. The parents would have been embarrassed. "Ms. Benson" would have blamed herself for allowing Jess to be in a position in which he could humiliate himself.

According to those who have overcome that fear of speaking to an audience, the way to conquer the fear is to do it—and then do it some more. The more often you speak before a group, the easier it becomes.

Ms. Benson could have insisted on giving Jess a non-speaking role in the play, but she was obliged to agree that he have a speaking part because he was brave enough to speak the lines before an audience. It is conceivable that some teachers in her place would have refused him, but they would be thinking more of the success of the play than of the mental health of their student.

An Activity Exploring Bravery

Most of us have little fears that plague us from time to time, but many of us have to confront those fears daily. We may be afraid that we won't say the right thing or will be embarrassed or that someone will discover a secret about us. Nevertheless, we deal with our fears and carry on.

Have students talk about times that they or someone they know displayed bravery. Try to keep the discussion centered on themselves or people they know, not celebrities or people in the news, so that students can see bravery in everyday life.

The Cartoon

Ms. Reynolds sat with a frown on her face, waiting for Maggie to come in after school. She looked up as a slender, attractive twelve-year-old girl opened the door and entered.

"What I wanted to talk to you about, Maggie," began Ms. Reynolds, "is something that has come up that troubles me greatly. Mrs. Williams phoned at noon and said she can't get Elise to go to school. Maybe you noticed she wasn't in class today."

"Oh, I guess I didn't notice, Ms. Reynolds," responded Maggie. "She doesn't talk to us girls very much."

"At any rate, something happened that pretty much shattered Elise, and her mother thinks you might know about it. Mrs. Williams and I just think that if there were an apology or some kind of gesture on the part of the individuals who did this thing to Elise that we could convince her to return to school tomorrow.

"It seems that one or more persons put a nasty cartoon in Elise's desk at noon yesterday when she was helping Mrs. Parsons with her first graders. From the description I was given, it was quite cruel. No wonder the girl is upset."

"Oh, that's too bad," ventured Maggie. "What was the cartoon like?"

"It showed a very obese girl with pimples eating Twinkies in her bedroom and saying: 'Tomorrow I'll get four more boxes. They don't last very long.'"

Maggie suppressed a smile, but Ms. Reynolds didn't notice.

"What makes Elise's mother think I know anything about it?" asked Maggie with an innocent look. "At noon, I was helping in the cafeteria kitchen."

"Elise told her mother that you must know about the cartoon," replied Ms. Reynolds. "Well, I guess you were working in the cafeteria when it must have happened, but you know what is going on, and I've always known you to tell the truth."

Elise was only too aware that Maggie didn't care for her. Maggie was either indifferent or unkind to Elise, and that may have been why she mentioned Maggie to her mother.

"I want to assure you, Maggie, that the people who did this won't be punished—although they should be. The idea is to try to get Elise not to feel so devastated by this prank. I know children can be cruel to one another, but I think if I can talk to the culprits I can convince them that playing that kind of joke on someone can have lasting effects."

"Yes, Ms. Reynolds," murmured Maggie.

The word *culprits* convinced Maggie not to say a word about her role in the prank. Elise had a good hunch that her tormentors were Maggie and a couple of her buddies, and she was right. Maggie had slipped out of the kitchen and met with Doris and Jeanna in the empty classroom. They had drawn the cartoon at Maggie's house the previous night, and they had waited till the classroom was empty to slip it into Elise's desk. Maggie was only gone from the kitchen for a few minutes.

"If you learn anything about this business, you'll let me know, won't you Maggie?"

"Yes, Ms. Reynolds," Maggie responded.

Name   **Date**

The Cartoon: Student Responses

Think about your answers to the following questions and write your response to each.

1. Why didn't Maggie confess that she was the ringleader of the girls who put the cartoon in Elise's desk?

_____

_____

_____

2. It would have taken courage for Maggie to confess. Would you have had that courage?

_____

_____

_____

3. Do you think that Ms. Reynolds guessed that Maggie was guilty?

_____

4. Does refusing to tell what happened make Maggie a coward? Why or why not?

_____

_____

_____

_____

For the Teacher

The Cartoon
Cowardice

The Story

There are various kinds of cowardice, but they are all prompted by or derive from fear—fear of the unknown; of physical harm; of social ostracism; of embarrassment, shame, or ridicule; of exposure or detection; and of loss of love, possessions, prestige, position, youth, reason (sanity), friendship, looks, and health.

Ms. Reynolds asked Maggie, who was the ringleader of the group of girls who played a prank on Elise, to give her any information she had about the cruel joke. According to her mother, Elise was so hurt that she didn't want to come to school anymore. Ms. Reynolds was under the impression that Maggie was helping in the cafeteria all during noon when a nasty cartoon was slipped into Elise's desk. When Mrs. Williams phoned Ms. Reynolds, she said that her daughter thought Maggie would know something about the prank. It is important that Ms. Reynolds knew who the students were who perpetrated the prank, not so she could punish them, but so she could persuade them to apologize to Elise. Maggie didn't admit to any knowledge of the prank. She was afraid that her standing with Ms. Reynolds and her classmates would suffer if she was exposed as a mean-spirited girl.

The Questions

Maggie didn't confess because she didn't want to be revealed as the instigator of the cruel prank. She was afraid that she would lose the respect of Ms. Reynolds and her classmates if it were known that she made fun of a fellow student.

The second question about the courage it takes to confess a misdeed gets at an uncomfortable point—namely, what percentage of twelve-year-olds would have confessed in this situation? Yes, it does take courage to admit you've done something as hurtful as Maggie and her friends did to another person.

It is certainly possible that Ms. Reynolds suspected Maggie of somehow being involved in the prank. From just reading the dialogue, however, it is hard to tell. Apparently Ms. Reynolds believed that Maggie was in the cafeteria all during the noon hour.

Your students have to determine whether or not Maggie acted cowardly by not confessing to her role in the incident. They could think that the word *cowardice* is too strong. Her silence can also be termed dishonest, and maybe that is as far as they would like to go in condemning Maggie. There isn't any question, however, that Maggie wasn't truthful or open with Ms. Reynolds about the prank, and so, yes, she acted in a cowardly way.

An Activity Exploring Cowardice

If students find Maggie to be a sufficiently memorable character, it might be both fun and instructive to have them look into literature to find a character that represents the epitome of a weak person who fails to do the right thing. There are a great many cowards in romantic novels, and there is no scarcity of moral weaklings in children's literature.

After they have searched and found their ideas of the "worst weakling," have your students look for the character in literature who is most unlike Maggie—someone who overcomes his or her fears and does the right thing. Give your students sufficient time to really look into the books. If they just pull names out of their head, challenge them with the names of other weak and/or courageous characters.

Student of the Week

Mr. Norton did his best to be evenhanded and fair with his twenty-seven sixth-grade students. First, he gave each student a turn at being "leader of the day," and that meant the student led in the flag salute, took the attendance slip to the office, had charge of the room's ventilation, and delivered messages for Mr. Norton. Second, he made sure that every student had a chance to be a monitor during the year; there were monitors for the balls, the lights, pets, plants, and paper distribution. Mr. Norton also made sure that the sides of teams during physical education were fair, occasionally playing on one side or another in games of volleyball, softball, and basketball. Sometimes he chose up the sides in order to avoid the procedure of having captains alternate in picking players and thus embarrassing the last students chosen.

This year he tried to encourage his average and below-average students by declaring a "Student of the Week" for each week of the school year. Mr. Norton calculated how much each student had improved in his or her scores during one week and then named the deserving student on Monday. He thought that he had done a good job of explaining to his students how the Student of the Week award worked and that it was intended to encourage those students who were most in need of improving (and thus not the top students), but he received a mild surprise during the week of parent-teacher conferences when he met with Susan Pearce's mother.

"Your daughter is performing very well, Mrs. Pearce," Mr. Norton began. "I really couldn't ask for anything more from her. She's conscientious, neat, and gets along well with all the boys and girls."

"Susan has always liked school, as I said in our last conference, but lately something has been bothering her. I think it must be this Student of the Week award."

"Oh," said Mr. Norton. "Maybe I understand."

"Yes, Mr. Norton. Here it is March, and you've had a great many Students of the Week, but Susan has never had the honor," complained Mrs. Pearce.

"I guess that's right. It goes to the student who has done the most improving during the week in his or her studies. I'm afraid that Susan doesn't have too much room for improvement," explained Mr. Norton.

"Don't you think that's unfair to the better students, Mr. Norton?"

"It does seem to be, all right, but I've tried to explain to the boys and girls that the award is really for encouraging those students who need to improve."

"Susan still thinks that by this time the better students should be Student of the Week—and I do too."

RESPONSES

Student of the Week: Student Responses

Think about your answers to the following questions and write your response to each.

1. Do you think that every student should have a chance to be a leader, as was the case in Mr. Norton's class? Why or why not?

_____

_____

_____

2. In his efforts to encourage his poorer students with the Student of the Week award, was Mr. Norton being fair? Explain.

_____

_____

_____

3. What could Mr. Norton have done so that the top students could occasionally be Student of the Week?

_____

_____

_____

4. Can any teacher be completely fair to all of his or her students? What makes you think so?

_____

_____

_____

Student of the Week
Fairness

The Story

As the last question at the end of the story hints, it is terrifically difficult for any teacher to be fair—and always appear to be fair—all of the time and in every way. Yet there are teachers whose students are convinced that their teachers are impartial and evenhanded with everyone in their classes. Mr. Norton thought that he had devised a system that was completely fair to his students. He may have erred, however, in giving the most prestigious award mostly to his less able students, thinking that this would be an incentive for them to improve their grades. It seemed fair to him, but one—and probably more—of his best students had other thoughts. Mr. Norton could either change the rules for determining the winners of the award or try to placate the disgruntled student and her mother. Mrs. Pearce, however, doesn't seem easily appeased.

The Questions

The first question is about Mr. Norton's policy of rotating students as monitors so that every student had the privilege and responsibilities of taking these jobs. Your students should see nothing wrong with his procedure. This question gets at the fact that Mr. Norton was a teacher who was very concerned about fairness.

Mr. Norton's way of determining a Student of the Week was his own invention. An innovative teacher, he tried out a number of new ideas every year. Mr. Norton hadn't established a Student of the Week award during the previous year, for instance. As Mrs. Pearce bluntly pointed out, the Student of the Week award was biased against the best students. Maybe it should have had another name, such as "Most Improved Student of the Week"; but if it had, some of the "punch" would have been taken from it.

Mr. Norton might have established another award if he didn't want to change the criteria for naming a Student of the Week. The danger in doing so, however, would be in exerting pressure on highly competitive students. He thought they were under enough pressure already.

All teachers can do is to try to be as fair as they can be, and Mr. Norton was doing a good job of that.

An Activity Exploring Fairness

After your students have discussed the story and answered the questions, hand out "Nobody Said" on page 94. This activity requires some guidance and tact on your part, however, because a couple of the questions will hit home. The title is from the too-familiar and cynical saying, "Nobody ever said that life is fair."

ACTIVITY

Name _____ **Date** _____

Nobody Said

An activity exploring fairness

Sometimes we find ourselves
saying, "It isn't fair!" And we
may be right. There are times
when prejudice, circumstances,
or superstition work hardships
on groups of people. Some
individuals definitely have
more obstacles to overcome
than others.

Write your thoughts on the lines below.

Is it fair that . . .

1. left-handed people have to sit at the left end of the dinner table?
Why or why not?

_____

_____

2. tiny women have to buy their clothes in the children's department?
Why or why not?

_____

_____

3. birds that are pretty and sing are put in cages? Why or why not?

_____

_____

4. the price of candy is three to five times higher than it was three
decades ago? Why or why not?

_____

_____

Name   Date

5. all the best parking places are reserved for persons with disabilities? Why or why not?

_____

_____

6. people have to buy licenses for their dogs but not for their cats? Why or why not?

_____

_____

7. there are more tall people heading corporations than short people? Why or why not?

_____

_____

8. teachers have a room to get away from their students, but students can't get away from their teachers in school? Why or why not?

_____

_____

9. there are neighborhoods that you can't get into without a resident's permission and others where hoodlums can drive through and shoot innocent people? Why or why not?

_____

_____

10. a conviction of drunk driving for adults is based on a measure of .08% alcohol in the blood, but only .01% for individuals younger than 21 years old? Why or why not?

_____

_____

Fred and Ted

Fred and Ted Swanson came into this world twenty months apart. His parents were deliriously happy when Fred arrived, but twenty months later they were just as happy when Ted made it a family of four. Mrs. Swanson had been the third of five daughters, and Mr. Swanson was an only child. They agreed that two sons were just fine with them.

As the boys grew up, they became quite different in their looks and personalities. Fred, who was pudgy and awkward, was moody at times and something of a bully, especially to Ted. He loved sports, but he wasn't particularly talented athletically. Ted, on the other hand, had a sunny disposition. He was a fine baseball player and the fastest runner in his class. He had become tall and coordinated.

The one recurring theme in the family's daily affairs—and it made life difficult for all four members—was the contention between the brothers. At first the parents tried to be fair and didn't assign blame to either boy when there was a scrap. Gradually, things got worse. When the boys were small, Fred was the obvious aggressor. As they reached the ages of eleven and a half and ten, Ted caught up in height. Fred then had a harder time getting the best of Ted physically, so he resorted to teasing. As a consequence, their parents began to blame Fred for any ruckus in the house. By the time they were thirteen and eleven and a half, Ted had begun finding ways of getting Fred's goat, becoming an expert at egging Fred on and getting him in trouble.

Mr. and Mrs. Swanson didn't have any experience with sibling rivalry. Mrs. Swanson and her sisters had gotten along quite well together, and Mr. Swanson hadn't had any siblings.

One day, Ted saw a chance to get his brother in real hot water.

"This will partly make up for all those poundings he gave me when we were little," thought Ted.

His parents were giving a big party, and his mother had baked two apple pies. Fred had a terrific appetite, and apple pie was absolutely his favorite food. Ted thought he could get away with a piece of pie and get Fred to grab a piece just before their mother returned from some last-minute shopping.

"If I can just time it right," he schemed, "he'll get it. Mom is due back from the supermarket any minute."

Ted came into Fred's room upstairs. "Smell something, Fred?" he asked.

"Yeah, smells good. I can smell it all the way up here. I think it's apple pie! Mom must have just baked it."

"I just had a hunk, and it's great," said Ted.

Fred went right down to the kitchen and located the two pies cooling on the counter, one missing a slice. Fred cut another wedge from that pie. He couldn't wait until he got the piece of pie into his room and took a big bite of it.

Just at that moment Mrs. Swanson came into the kitchen with her arms full of groceries. She almost dropped the bags when she saw Fred with the slice of pie.

"What do you think you're doing, young man?" she gasped. "That pie is for the party tonight!"

"Oh, gosh, Mom. I forgot about the party," Fred stammered.

"You're grounded for a month, Fred!" his mother half-shouted.

"But, Mom, look there," Fred said, pointing to the pie, "Ted had a piece before I did."

"How do I know that? I can see bits of the pie in the corners of your mouth. Don't blame Ted for your gluttony, Fred," retorted Mrs. Swanson.

Ted denied ever having seen the pies, and so Fred was grounded for a month.

RESPONSES

Name   Date

Fred and Ted: Student Responses

Think about your answers to the following questions and write your response to each.

1. Do the Swansons show favoritism in the way they treat their sons?

_____

2. Fred can't beat Ted up anymore, and if he tries to get even in another way he is likely to get in trouble all over again. What, if anything, will he do to Ted for pulling this trick on him?

_____

_____

_____

3. What will this experience do to Fred, who is rather moody anyway?

_____

_____

_____

4. If you were Mr. or Mrs. Swanson, how would you try to help the boys get along better?

_____

_____

_____

5. Will Fred ever be treated fairly by his parents, or will they always favor Ted?

_____

_____

_____

Fred and Ted
Unfairness

The Story

Fairness is one of the most desirable qualities in a parent or a teacher. Universally, young people want those in authority to be fair in their dealings with them. It's only natural. Because most parents want to treat their children fairly, some are surprised when a grown child claims his or her parents always favored a sibling. To conscientious parents who had tried not to favor one child over another, the accusation can be startling. Nevertheless, in the story about Fred and Ted, the boys' parents favored the younger brother, Ted. It may have been because of his personality or his looks, but Ted was definitely the favorite.

The Questions

The first question concerning favoritism is really rhetorical and is intended to get your students thinking about the inequities in the Swanson family. Obviously, the boys' parents favored Ted over Fred.

The second question has to do with retribution or retaliation, one of the world's most depressing problems. One group seems to always want to seek revenge against another, as demonstrated almost daily in particular countries around the world. Probably the best way for Fred to deal with the experience is to try to forget it—but a month is a long time when you are thirteen.

This experience won't make Fred any happier—that's for sure. In fact, it is the kind of experience that people tend to remember for the rest of their lives. Ted seems to be getting the best of him, and the relationship between the brothers is only getting worse. Your students' reactions to this question should be revealing, especially from those who have brothers and/or sisters.

Your students' suggestions about ameliorating the situation could be worth noting. When a family can't resolve this kind of problem, it can fester and lead to some serious consequences.

If there is genuine favoritism, as there seems to be, Fred will continue to suffer. He will probably have to adjust and not dwell on the difference in his parents' treatment of the two, if possible.

For the Teacher

From *Exploring Character*, Copyright © Good Year Books. This page may be reproduced for classroom use only by the actual purchaser of the book. www.goodyearbooks.com.

An Activity Exploring Unfairness

It is very important to young people that others be fair to them, and they also want things generally to be fair—not biased or inequitable—in life. "Fair or Foul?" on page 101 asks students to examine situations that may seem unfair but are really not. By thinking hard about each situation, your students can find a reason for calling it "fair."

Following are some ways in which the eight situations presented in the activity can be construed as being "fair":

1. Nature seems to be cruel at times. The parent birds don't mind the biggest chick getting most of the food because that will ensure that one healthy chick will survive.

2. It's not fair to others for someone with a communicable disease to be in a group of people. It's only fair that the individual isn't able to pass those germs along to others.

3. The teacher probably has her reasons for selecting the boy to open the windows. He may not be good at performing other little chores in the classroom, and his ego gets a boost from doing this one.

4. To hungry students in the upper grades, knowing the primary children eat first in the cafeteria is annoying, but the schedule of primary children is usually different and they leave school earlier, thus necessitating the early lunch time.

5. The younger sibling will have to pay when he or she reaches his or her sibling's age a year later.

6. Many teachers still use the alphabet as a guide in organizing their students in various ways. The reason this can be quite fair is that sometimes it is desirable to be among the first.

7. The unfairness about hand-me-downs is that the first-born boy or girl doesn't have to put up with wearing used clothes that others have seen on his or her siblings. The fairness in large families is that all but the first-born know that their siblings must also wear hand-me-downs. In big families of modest means, that is the way it is.

8. This is the fix that all inexperienced people have when they are seeking employment. If the job calls for experience as one of its qualifications, it seems impossible (and unfair) to the applicant because he or she is simply trying to get the job—and thus experience. Without ever getting hired, the applicant can never be qualified. It is only fair if the applicant can work into the job from another position, as so often happens.

Name	Date

Fair or Foul?

An activity exploring unfairness

There are many things in life that appear to be unfair, but are actually fair. On the lines below, tell why each of the following situations really is fair:

1. The biggest chick in a nest consistently pushes the other chicks out of the way and gets almost all of the food that the parent birds bring to the nest, thus starving the other nestlings.

_____

_____

_____

2. A boy or girl gets the chicken pox and can't go to school on "All Sports Day."

_____

_____

_____

3. A teacher always asks a tall boy to open the upper windows of her classroom. She doesn't ask other students who are almost as tall as he is.

_____

_____

_____

Activity

Name   Date

4. Primary children get to go to the cafeteria and the older kids, who are a lot hungrier, have to wait until later.

_____

_____

_____

5. The younger brother or sister gets into an amusement park free, but the sibling who is only a year older has to pay.

_____

_____

_____

6. Someone whose name starts with A has to sit in the front row and be called on a lot, whereas someone whose name starts with W sits in the back and can duck behind another student.

_____

_____

_____

7. A younger brother or sister has to wear a hand-me-down jacket because his or her mother says, "It is perfectly good and it fits fine."

_____

_____

_____

8. A local druggist puts a sign in his store's window declaring he needs help, but when you inquire about the job he says that you must have experience. How can you gain experience if you first have to have it in order to get the job?

_____

_____

_____

Friends and Relatives

"That's a really nice sweater, Becky. I haven't seen it before. How long have you had it?" asked Tanya.

"Oh, not very long. I got it for Christmas. My uncle sent it from Central America. Guatemala, I think it was," replied Becky.

"I have one a little like it, but it came from Mexico. One of my older cousins sent it. My relatives there are good to me. Even though they have lots of relatives in the United States, they never forget my birthday," Tanya said proudly.

"You're lucky, Tanya. I don't hear from my cousins very often. They're not so far away, either, but they're all on my dad's side—my mom was an only child—and my dad's brothers and sisters aren't close to one another."

"You know, Becky, I really *am* lucky. My cousins in Mexico keep telling me so, but they don't have to convince me. My brothers and sisters and I get along pretty well, although we fight every now and then. My older brother, for instance."

"Yeah, my sister and I fight sometimes, too. She can be a pain," said Becky.

"Well, my brother and I really didn't have a fight. We just quarreled about who had better teachers. He thinks because he's in high school that his teachers are better, but we have the best teachers. Everybody says Mr. Mitchell is the best teacher around, and Ms. Nesbitt is terrific, too. My parents think I'm lucky to be in this school."

"I suppose so," offered Becky.

"I heard Tom say that our class is something special, too. He says he wouldn't want to be in any other class. I felt that way the other day in Dance Club. The kids in our club really stick up for you—not that anyone is giving us a bad time. When I needed a green scarf to go with my new outfit for the dance, Christina found out and asked if I'd like to borrow hers. Once Tom walked 2-1/2 miles to my house after school to give me a homework assignment when I was sick. I love coming to school. My cousins say I should be grateful. They're happy when they have enough pencils to use in school."

Name   **Date**

Friends and Relatives: Student Responses

Think about your answers to the following questions and write your response to each.

1. Do you feel the same way about your friends at school as Tanya does? Why or why not?

_____

_____

_____

2. Is Tanya going to be disappointed in her teachers and friends when she gets to high school? Why do you think so?

_____

_____

_____

3. Do you know anyone like Tom, who walked 2-1/2 miles to give Tanya a homework assignment? Who is it?

_____

_____

_____

4. Does being in a club promote generosity in its members? Why or why not?

_____

_____

_____

For the Teacher

Friends and Relatives
Gratitude

The Story

Reading the dialogue between Tanya and Becky, your students can tell that Tanya is a happy and grateful girl. She experiences love at home and also at school. There can't be a better feeling than knowing you are well loved. Perhaps because her background is different, Becky doesn't seem so enthusiastic about her lot in life, but she is aware that she has a lot to be grateful for. As a Mexican American, Tanya is often confronted with the contrast between her life and that of her cousins south of the border.

The Questions

Tanya really is lucky. She is thoroughly satisfied with her life at home and at school. If a majority of your students can identify with her, you have a good teaching situation.

There is no way of knowing whether a happy, well-adjusted student in middle school will be as happy and well-adjusted in high school, but the odds are in her favor because she has a positive outlook. Actually, the middle school years are usually considered more troublesome for young people.

Anyone, young or old, is fortunate when she or he has someone like Tom for a friend. We can usually count our Tom-like friends on one hand.

Some clubs try to promote consideration for other club members. The idea that club members should be loyal and true is specifically stated in creeds. Whether or not clubs promote generosity is another question.

An Activity Exploring Gratitude

"Good Feelings" on page 107 is the kind of activity that can produce a wealth of information about your students. However, you must handle it with care to preserve students' privacy and to elicit honest answers.

Allow students plenty of time to respond in private. Keep the discussion positive. Obviously the student who has trouble coming up with responses about things to be grateful about is one who probably has some problems—or is hopelessly spoiled.

Name	Date

Good Feelings

An activity exploring gratitude

Most of us are lucky enough to be grateful for a number of blessings. Below, write what you are most grateful about when it comes to:

1. your friendships:

_____

_____

Why? _____

_____

2. your family:

_____

_____

Why? _____

_____

3. the entertainment available to you:

_____

_____

Why? _____

_____

4. your opportunities for learning:

_____

_____

Why? _____

_____

ACTIVITY

Name   Date

5. your special talents:

_____

_____

Why? _____

_____

6. your neighborhood or community:

_____

_____

Why? _____

_____

7. your country:

_____

_____

Why? _____

_____

8. your beliefs:

_____

_____

Why? _____

_____

Of all the things you are grateful for, which one gives you the best feeling?

_____

The Jacket

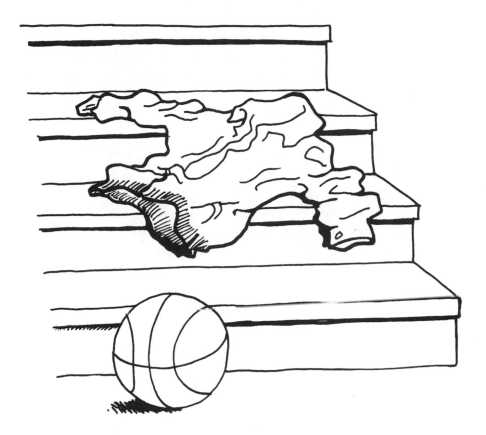

Marcus and Ryan were the last ones out of the gym one cold and windy January afternoon. They'd been practicing with the basketball team, which was preparing for a game the next day with Orono Middle School, their chief rival in the league.

"Say, isn't that Eugene's jacket over there in the stands?" asked Ryan.

"I think so, but I'm not sure," answered Marcus.

"Maybe we'd better pick it up for him. Someone might take it home, and it looks like a pretty good jacket," said Ryan. "He'll want it tomorrow because we're supposed to get a heavy rainstorm. I think I'll pick it up for him. He only lives six blocks from my house."

Ryan went into the stands and picked up Eugene's jacket. Then he and Marcus walked briskly out of the gym and took different routes home. Marcus, who lived farther away from school, had a bike; but

Ryan had left his bike at home because it had a bent front rim as a result of a crash he'd had last week. As he walked home, with the wind in his face, Ryan called himself a couple of names for not repairing his bike several days ago.

About three blocks from where he usually turned off the main street to go home, Ryan kept going, and it wasn't long before he reached Eugene's house. He rang the doorbell. As it happened, Eugene answered the doorbell.

"Hi, Eugene. I think you left this at the gym. You may be needing it," Ryan said.

"Yeah, it's mine. Okay. I've got another one. See ya," Eugene said, closing the door.

Ryan hesitated a second on the doorstep, and then turned and trotted in the direction of his house. A blast of cold wind cut through his jacket and chilled his chest. He felt a little empty. "Oh, well," he said to himself.

Name _____ **Date** _____

The Jacket: Student Responses

Think about your answers to the following questions and write your response to each.

1. Should Ryan have bothered to walk those extra blocks to give Eugene his jacket? Explain your answer.

_____

_____

_____

_____

2. If you had been Eugene, how would you have shown your appreciation for what Ryan did?

_____

_____

_____

3. Do you think this incident will discourage Ryan from doing favors for people in the future? Why or why not?

_____

_____

_____

4. Why didn't Eugene thank Ryan?

_____

_____

_____

For the Teacher

From *Exploring Character*, Copyright © Good Year Books. This page may be reproduced for classroom use only by the actual purchaser of the book. www.goodyearbooks.com.

The Jacket
Ingratitude

The Story

We don't mind going out of our way and doing favors for people if what we do is appreciated. When we get a "brush-off," we feel a little betrayed. Ryan decided that he'd do a good deed and take Eugene's jacket to his house. Eugene didn't even thank him, remarking that he had another jacket. That's not only ungrateful—it's rude.

The Questions

Ryan didn't expect Eugene to be so indifferent about getting his jacket back. Ryan was trying to be thoughtful because he believed Eugene would certainly need his jacket when it rained the next day. Many good-hearted students would probably do the same.

At least Eugene could have thanked Ryan for going to the trouble of bringing him the coat. He treated Ryan as if he were a bother. If his response to Ryan is typical of his behavior, he has deplorable manners.

It's debatable as to how the incident will affect Ryan. He may be a little reluctant to go out of his way to do someone a favor in the future, but we doubt it. It is his nature to be thoughtful and helpful—but he probably won't jump to help Eugene again.

The question underlying the end of the story is why Eugene didn't thank Ryan for going out of his way to deliver the jacket to Eugene. Your students may think that he is spoiled, or thoughtless, or naturally ungracious, or the kind of person who expects others to go out of their way for him.

An Activity Exploring Ingratitude

Ask students to write about an episode in their lives in which they were thoughtful of someone else, but that thoughtfulness was not appreciated. If your students are lucky enough to have never personally experienced ingratitude, have them write a fictional story describing an incident like that in "The Jacket."

Trudy Tells All

Mrs. Templeton's class this year had been one she would always remember. Her sixth graders had included Wes, who had defeated every teacher before Mrs. Templeton, and even she could only claim a draw at the end of the year. Another boy, Jeff, was eager, smart, and a joy to teach. Tara was a talented athlete but an indifferent student. There were also Bobby and Jake and David—all handfuls.

And then there was Trudy. A twelve-year-old of average size who had a pleasant, slightly freckled face, Trudy was not shy, but she was not very forward either. Although her classwork wasn't outstanding, she worked very well with others in committees and happily took on any assignment. Trudy's most distinguishing characteristic was an open smile that revealed a trusting and loving nature.

In the middle of the year Mrs. Templeton had come under fire. Jake was disgruntled because he wasn't the leader that he had been in the fifth grade, and he blamed Mrs. Templeton. He had been nominated for a class office five times and had never won. In addition, Jake's mother believed Mrs. Templeton gave students too much freedom in the classroom. Because Jake's family lived near Trudy's, Jake's mother came over to question Trudy about Mrs. Templeton.

"Does she let you kids get out of your seats when you want to?" asked Jake's mother.

"Oh, yes, if there is a reason to get up," answered Trudy.

"Doesn't that cause a lot of confusion, Trudy?"

"Sometimes. Especially if Wes is one of the people out of his seat," replied Trudy.

"Do you think anyone is learning anything?"

"Sure. We learn a lot. Mrs. Templeton just has a different way of teaching than Mrs. Carter did last year."

Jake's mother came away from the interview with a clear picture of Mrs. Templeton's classroom and her role there.

By the end of the year Jake had had some successes and was mildly praising Mrs. Templeton at home. In the last faculty meeting, the principal made a veiled reference to parents who had been highly critical of Mrs. Templeton but who were now boosters. It was likely that Trudy's candid replies to Jake's mother's questions had forestalled a determined campaign against Mrs. Templeton. She never knew that Trudy's innocent responses had saved her a good deal of grief.

Name _____   Date _____

Trudy Tells All: Student Responses

Think about your answers to the following questions and write your response to each.

1. Do you know any "Trudys"? If so, are they popular?

_____

_____

_____

2. What might have happened if Trudy had been less open in her statements about Mrs. Templeton?

_____

_____

_____

3. What role do you think the principal played in the business of Jake's mother's criticism of Mrs. Templeton? What makes you think so?

_____

_____

_____

4. Was Jake's mother justified in questioning Mrs. Templeton's teaching methods? Why or why not?

_____

_____

_____

For the Teacher

Trudy Tells All
Openness

The Story

In many schools the parents take a very active role in what goes on. Mrs. Templeton's school was in an older neighborhood, and the people there liked to know all about the teachers and students there. Moreover, Jake's mother was a lot like a growing contingent of parents who think that anything that goes wrong for their son or daughter at school is the school's fault. They don't look for deficiencies in their children, and many ignore the possibility that their child is to blame in any situation.

The Questions

A Trudy tends to be quite popular. Her kind of open, trusting nature is one that nearly all of us prefer to more unpredictable and closed personalities. It's comfortable being around a Trudy. You don't have to be on your guard.

If Trudy had been an evasive person, Jake's mother might very well have thought there was something seriously wrong in Mrs. Templeton's classroom. The point of this question is that when we are even a little bit evasive, people tend to become suspicious and imagine things are not what they should be.

At the end of the story, your students learn that the principal saw fit to mention that Mrs. Templeton had had her critics. They can guess that during the year he was well aware of the feelings of Jake's mother regarding Mrs. Templeton.

The fourth question deals with the issue of parents going to school to ensure that their children are being treated fairly. There are certainly occasions when parents should go to the administration and determine whether a student has been mistreated. Your students' responses may very well be mixed. How does a student feel if a parent complains to the principal or teacher?

An Activity Exploring Openness

You might follow up the story about Trudy with a writing activity concerning a boy similar to Trudy. With the entire class, decide on a setting for the story (locale of the community, type of school, grade of the main character, etc.) and the time (today, in the recent past, or in the future). Then ask for some ideas about the personality of this male counterpart of Trudy. He doesn't have to be Trudy's age (twelve) or have her temperament, but he should have her endearing quality of being open and honest.

Naturally each student will have his or her own ideas for a plot. Tell your students that they shouldn't be influenced by "Trudy Tells All" (which is largely a true story, by the way). Ask them to give a good deal of thought to the special problem that open, guileless people have. They do tend to overcome these problems.

The New Teacher

The school year was just two weeks old, and things hadn't settled down yet in Mr. Carmichael's sixth-grade classroom. Mr. Carmichael was new to their school, and some students were still trying to figure him out. Their fifth-grade teacher, Mrs. Stafford, had been very different. She was a very traditional teacher, and her students always knew what to expect.

On the first day of sixth grade, Mr. Carmichael had shocked his twenty-five students by telling them to sit wherever they liked. He had only one rule: You had to be courteous to everyone and be considerate of their rights and feelings. Outside the room, at the end of the day, Jake and James and a few others said aloud what they thought the year was going to be like.

"Easy!" exclaimed James.

"Yeah, easy!" echoed Jake.

Teresa and some of the girls were surprised to find out that although they had always sat in rows, now they sat in circles of three and four most of the time. They used to march to the cafeteria in lines, but now they walked informally. They used to take a pretest and a final test in spelling each week, but now they gave each other tests of words they wanted to learn to spell.

"I've never had a teacher like him," Teresa declared with a frown.

Jeff thought that they ought to withhold their judgment of Mr. Carmichael. "He's different, all right, and maybe he's not as good as Mrs. Stafford," said Jeff, "but let's see how it goes. He seems like a good guy."

By the second Friday, the class was divided. Some were unhappy with the lack of structure in their lessons and routine, but some liked their new freedom. Mr. Carmichael posted the day's schedule on the chalkboard each day, but he rarely stuck to it. If a discussion got going on a topic, he might ignore the next subject on the schedule; or if a project in science or art went well, it might go on all afternoon.

Mr. Carmichael did win some points with his students when he entered into the volleyball game in the physical education period and later talked about major league baseball. (Mrs. Stafford didn't know anything about baseball.)

"We'll have a good year if we go along with Mr. Carmichael and his ideas," Jeff told some of his classmates after school that week. "We're used to one kind of teacher, and he's just not that kind, but let's see if we learn anything this year."

The others seemed to agree with Jeff, nodding their heads and saying "Uh-huh."

"Yeah, you're right, Jeff," said James. "Mr. Carmichael's not like Mrs. Stafford, but his ways might be all right."

Name   Date

The New Teacher: Student Responses

Think about your answers to the following questions and write your response to each.

1. Have you ever had trouble adjusting to a teacher who was different? What happened?

_____

_____

_____

2. Do you think any of the students in Mr. Carmichael's class complained about him to Mrs. Stafford? Why or why not?

_____

_____

3. Jeff insisted that the kids keep open minds regarding Mr. Carmichael's methods. If Jeff had made up his mind that Mr. Carmichael was a very poor teacher, what do you think would have happened that year?

_____

_____

_____

4. Do you suppose Mr. Carmichael had some expectations of his students? Could he have been disappointed in his students? Do teachers have to keep an open mind about their students? Explain.

_____

_____

_____

_____

_____

For the Teacher

The New Teacher
Open-mindedness

The Story

In the story about the new teacher (who was new only to the school and not to teaching), your students are asked to see both sides of a problem. They may or may not identify with the students who were uncomfortable with Mr. Carmichael's style, but they can probably understand that many of his students wished that they still had Mrs. Stafford. In contradistinction, your students are also asked to sympathize with Mr. Carmichael's efforts to teach in his own way, as advocated by Jeff. The impact of having a different kind of teacher for the current school year was also felt by the parents, and in this case the parents did get into the act, especially one mother. It happened that the community in which the school was located was especially conservative. Nevertheless, Mr. Carmichael knew something of the school, the principal, and the students before the school year began.

The Questions

Until students enter middle school (or junior high), they may not have to do a great deal of adjusting to their teachers. Often the transition from the primary to the intermediate grades goes smoothly, especially in schools with little turnover of staff. After entering middle school, however, one of their toughest tasks is to adjust to the changing of classrooms and teachers. Accordingly, if your students are in middle school, they most likely will be able to cite one or two times when adjusting to a teacher was difficult.

The second question may be quite revealing with regard to your students' personalities, and their answers will depend upon their own tendencies to complain about things. Complaining to a former teacher about the present one has been known to happen.

Without Jeff's support, Mr. Carmichael's first month or so could have been much rockier.

Teachers do have preconceptions about classes, as well as individuals. Mr. Carmichael may have heard what a wonderful group he was to teach, and he might have become very disappointed to find that the students were not as well-behaved or adventurous as he'd been led to believe. Teachers should keep an open mind, too.

An Activity Exploring Open-mindedness

Once your students have explored the ideas and issues in "The New Teacher," hand out "Judgments" on page 121. You can administer it individually or to the entire class.

ACTIVITY

Name

Date

Judgments

An activity exploring open-mindedness

Do you sometimes make a judgment about someone or something in a hurry? Actually, everybody does, even when there is time to think about whether or not the judgment is sound. Sometimes, however, we should take some time to get more information about the matter at hand.

Read the descriptions below. In which of these situations might you want more information before making a judgment? In which of the situations would you probably have no need for further information? On the lines below, explain your reasoning.

1. Choosing a person to sit next to:

_____

_____

2. Purchasing a sweater for everyday wear:

_____

_____

3. Deciding whether a stairway is safe to climb:

_____

_____

_____

4. Getting a new or used bicycle:

_____

_____

ACTIVITY

Name   Date

5. Tuning in to a TV program for the first time:

_____

_____

_____

6. Drinking the water from the tap in your kitchen:

_____

_____

_____

7. Selecting a new pair of shoes:

_____

_____

_____

8. Turning in a joke to the editor of the school newspaper:

_____

_____

_____

9. Deciding whether to accept a ride from someone you barely know:

_____

_____

_____

10. Purchasing a birthday gift for a friend:

_____

_____

_____

Pie

"Oh, I wish they wouldn't play that music in here!" Shannon protested in the bookstore.

"Why?" Ashley asked.

"It's awful! I hate classical music!" exclaimed Shannon. "It gets on my nerves."

"I've heard my dad say the same thing about the music we like," returned Ashley.

"Anyway—let's get out of here, Ashley. I can't take that music anymore."

The girls left the bookstore and its recorded chamber music and walked toward the mall. On the way, they strolled in front of a restaurant. There was a menu posted outside, and they paused to read it.

"My mom and dad think this is a great place to eat," commented Ashley. "They say it's famous for its great desserts, especially their pies."

"Can't stand it!" said Shannon.

"What?" asked Ashley.

"Pie. I never eat it."

"Really now, Shannon. What's wrong with pie? There are all kinds of pie—apple, chocolate, lemon meringue, pecan, pumpkin, and a whole lot more."

"Never eat 'em," said Shannon.

"Haven't you *ever* eaten a piece of pie?" asked Ashley.

"No. When I was little, my mother tried to get me to eat a piece of one, but I wouldn't."

"You mean you've never tasted pie?" asked Ashley in genuine surprise.

"I knew I wouldn't like it, so I didn't eat it," explained Shannon.

"Oh," sighed Ashley.

Name   **Date**

Pie: Student Responses

Think about your answers to the following questions and write your response to each.

1. Is there some food that you have never tasted? If so, what is it?

_____

_____

2. Is there some food that you don't like and won't eat? If so, what is it?

_____

_____

3. It seems that Shannon has some very definite opinions about what she likes and what she doesn't like. Do you know anyone like that? What are they set against?

_____

_____

_____

4. Do you think that Shannon is going to miss out on any good experiences in life if she doesn't become more open to new things? Explain.

_____

_____

_____

_____

Pie
Prejudice and close-mindedness

The Story

There are a lot of Shannons in the world. They make a snap judgment about something and rarely change their minds. Although pie would seem to be appealing, there are people such as "Shannon" who grow up refusing to eat it or some other food item. There are probably more people who don't like classical music. We enjoy both, to the utmost.

The Questions

If we are not mistaken, there will be students in your class who refuse to eat cauliflower, broccoli, lima beans, mince pie, eggplant, or yams—but probably no one who refuses to eat junk food. Many of the foods that they won't touch will be good for them, but they've heard that argument before. Your students will very much enjoy discussing all the foods they can't stand.

The point of the story is that Shannon is closed-minded. Once she decides she doesn't like something, it is nearly impossible to get her to change her mind. It's too bad, too. Often an adult will try cauliflower and discover that he or she really does enjoy it, especially with a good cream or cheese sauce. As for pie, the people who won't taste it are beyond hope!

People like Shannon undoubtedly miss out on a lot. They form very quick opinions—which become hardened prejudices—about hairstyles, television personalities, furniture, political figures, ethnic groups, art, religious sects, and countless other subjects. Of course there are times when they regret a snap judgment they have made, but that doesn't stop them from continuing to make these judgments. Educators, however, can show the advantages of having an open mind.

An Activity Exploring Closed-mindedness

Shannon has no information about how she might like a piece of pie because she has never eaten a piece of pie. Without any experiences eating one or more pieces of pie, she can't make a rational judgment about pies.

This kind of closed-mindedness extends into dealings with people as well. Too often someone will say that they don't like an entire group of people. When asked if he or she has ever spoken to a member of that group, the response, regrettably, is often *no*. However, he or she is quite certain that the whole group is not to be trusted.

"Decisions" on page 127 will encourage your students to seek more information in cases in which their decisions about trying something new may have long-term consequences. Add any other situations in which you think they should hesitate and then try to get more information before making a decision. Taking drugs or drinking alcohol are not on the list, but that may be one you'd like to add to our list.

Name   Date

VANILLA
STRAWBERRY
CHOCO RIFFIC
CRUNCHY NUT
TUTTI-FRUTTI
MONGO MANGO
BUTTER RIPPLE
MELLOW MALLOW
COFFEE TOFFEE
COTTON CANDY
STICKY SUNDAE

GROOVY GRAPE
CRAZY CARAMEL
KOOKY COOKIE
ESPRESSO MOCHA
FUNNY FUDGE
BUBBLE GUM
PEPPERMINT STICK
CREME ANGLAISE
JUMPING BEAN
SILLY STR
PURPLE PA

Decisions

An activity exploring closed-mindedness

Have you ever made a quick decision about someone or something? Below are a variety of matters about which young people commonly have to make decisions. Put the number of each situation in one of the three columns on the following page: those for which more information is needed, those for which you are not sure you need more information, and those for which you have sufficient information to make a decision. Then answer the questions that follow.

1. Whether to rent a new video you've heard mentioned by a friend

2. Whether to join a group that is going to go whitewater rafting

3. Which flavor of ice cream to order

4. Whether or not to wear rain gear in the morning

5. Which person to invite to go with you on a family outing

6. Whether to volunteer to be on a committee at school

7. Whether to take a French or a Spanish class

ACTIVITY

From *Exploring Character*, Copyright © Good Year Books. This page may be reproduced for classroom use only by the actual purchaser of the book. www.goodyearbooks.com.

_____   _____
Name   Date

8. Whether to pass along some gossip about a friend

9. Whether to take a second helping of food

10. Whether to stay up and watch another program

11. Whether to "tell" on your brother or sister

12. Whether to ask a question when you don't understand the teacher

I should get more information about these:	I'm not sure if I need more information about these:	I have all the information I need about these:

Have you had to make decisions about any of the above dilemmas recently? If so, which ones?

_____

_____

What kinds of decisions are especially hard for you to make?

_____

_____

Penny's Story

Penny always had trouble expressing herself in writing. She didn't have much of a problem in expressing herself when she talked, but when she tried to write a story or a report, she couldn't put the words down in a clear, understandable way. It was especially hard for her to think of an idea for a story and then get it down on paper, or even on a computer. That's why Penny's heart sank one Monday when Mr. Conrad asked the class to write an original story. She didn't like to ask others for help, but story ideas just didn't come to her easily.

"I can't think of anything for a story," Penny said to Mr. Conrad at the end of the period. "Do I have to write a story? Can I write a report or something instead?"

"Oh, you can do it, Penny," he replied. "It may take you a while to get an idea, but I'm sure one will come to you. Just let your imagination take over."

Penny wasn't convinced it would be that easy. She said, "Thanks, Mr. Conrad. I'll try." The stories were to be turned in on Friday.

That night at dinner Penny complained to her family.

"I've got another story to write. We can write about anything—it can be any kind of story. That's the worse kind. If the teachers would give us a topic or a problem, it would be a lot easier."

"Would you like some help, Penny?" George, her older brother, asked kindly. "I can give you a couple of ideas. I had Mr. Conrad, and I think I know what he likes."

"No thanks, George. I have to use my own ideas—not that I have any—but I appreciate your offer."

Penny was like that. She was independent and wanted to earn her own way. For a couple of days she struggled with writing her story. She wrote two, but they were short and also, she thought, stupid. She wrote another, which was a little longer, and took it to her mother.

"Would you please read this, Mom? I don't think it is any good, but tomorrow I have to hand in *something*."

Penny's mother sat down at the dining room table and concentrated on reading the story. She frowned a little and then gave a sigh.

"Well, it's original, Penny. I'll say that. But the ending is pretty flat. There's no sense of solving anything. I think you've made a start."

The expression on Penny's face was pained. "Okay, Mom. That's a good criticism. I didn't like the ending either."

So Penny rewrote the ending. "There. Maybe that's a little better," she said to herself. "I'll ask George what he thinks."

George was somewhat encouraging. "It's okay, but try using a few more action verbs, Penny. The story moves a little slowly, if you know what I mean. Mr. Conrad likes stories to be colorful and to move along."

This time Penny was really downcast. She couldn't bring herself to rewrite the story again. But, after an hour of sulking, she did. It took a lot of determination on her part to do it, though.

When the stories were graded and returned to the students, she was thrilled to get a B– and this comment from Mr. Conrad: "I knew you could do it, Penny."

Name   Date

Penny's Story: Student Responses

Think about your answers to the following questions and write your response to each.

1. Do you like to write a story for a teacher without being told what it should be about? Why or why not?

_____

_____

_____

2. Do you know anyone like Penny who tries hard and doesn't give up? Do you admire that quality in a person? Explain.

_____

_____

_____

3. What kind of job might Penny be good at when she graduates? Explain why she would be good at it.

_____

_____

_____

4. How much help should a student get from other students and from adults in writing a story? Is it all right to get suggestions but not all right to have another person help you write a story?

_____

_____

_____

_____

For the Teacher

Penny's Story
Persistence

The Story

Not much gets accomplished without effort. In some cases nothing gets done at all. Some teachers give grades for effort. Why should there be a grade for effort? Are we assuming that the average student doesn't put out enough effort? Penny was certainly not in that category. Persistent effort enabled her to complete a job satisfactorily, even though it was one she very much disliked.

Evidently Penny isn't imaginative. When her teacher assigned a story but gave no hint about what the story was to be about, Penny was unhappy. But Penny has a quality that is prized by teachers, parents, and employers—persistence. Through pluck and hard work (writing is work), she was finally able to write a fairly good story. Penny didn't want anyone's help because she is an independent, self-sufficient young lady, but the two suggestions by her mother and brother enabled her to produce an acceptable story.

The Questions

Many students like to have structure in all of their school work and feel quite uncomfortable when told to use their imaginations. Penny would have preferred that Mr. Conrad specify a theme or subject or perhaps a problem to be solved. Leaving it wide open was the exact opposite of what Penny wanted. Some of your students will probably sympathize with her point of view.

It is possible that someone in your class is like Penny and that his or her fellow students recognize the fact. Guide students in seeing the positive aspects of Penny. There should be nothing negative associated with a student's resembling Penny.

We need the Pennys to carry out countless tasks in society. The "I won't give up" attitude is needed in the fields of social work, teaching, medicine, invention (Thomas Edison is the familiar model of persistence), rescue work, athletics, engineering, architecture, and criminal investigation, to name a few. Penny would be a valuable worker in any of these fields.

The fourth question brings up a tricky problem for both teachers and students. We know that many parents do help their children with their homework. We do know that some parents actually do the writing or computation. Some of that help is good and necessary. Some is not and is basically wrong. Penny has the idea that the work must be her own and doesn't allow her brother to help her.

An Activity Exploring Persistence

The issue of trying hard in order to be successful has long been a critical one in our society. Generally speaking, we've endorsed the notion that if an individual will just try harder he or she will succeed. "Some Signs of Success" on page 133 will give your students a chance to determine how we judge success in our society.

Name   **Date**

Some Signs of Success

An activity exploring persistence

Success can be described in a great many ways—winning a game or a championship, being happy with your family, making enough money to retire at age fifty, being listed in *Who's Who*, doing well in your job and being promoted, having your business grow and making a lot of money, losing ten pounds or reaching some other goal, completing a crossword puzzle, finding a cure for a disease, and being named a blue ribbon winner at the fair, among many, many others.

Are any of the following signs of success? Explain why or why not.

(Sign in a restaurant) IN GOD WE TRUST—ALL OTHERS PAY CASH:

_____

_____

(Announcement on a TV screen) TECHNICAL DIFFICULTIES—PLEASE STAND BY:

_____

_____

(Sign in a window of a house) ROOM FOR RENT:

_____

_____

ACTIVITY

Name   Date

(Sign in the window of a grocery store) HELP WANTED—APPLY WITHIN:

_____

_____

(Ad in a newspaper) CELEBRATING 25 YEARS OF DOING BUSINESS:

_____

_____

(Sign in a barber shop window) GONE FISHIN':

_____

_____

(Sign on a fence) NO TRESPASSING:

_____

_____

How do *you* define success?

_____

_____

_____

_____

_____

Roger the Dodger

R oger's Uncle Harry owned the town's only lumberyard. In September, Roger had his eye on a computer game that was on sale at Weinstein's electronics store. Unfortunately for Roger, he was broke. Then he thought of his uncle. Somehow he talked his uncle into paying him in advance for a day's work at the lumberyard, saying that the computer game wouldn't be on sale by the following Saturday, when he'd do the work.

Roger, however, was not fond of working hard. The last time he had worked at the lumberyard he had come home bone-tired. He was not looking forward to going back.

When Saturday rolled around, Roger showed up a few minutes late to start the work he owed his uncle. He then began unloading shingles from two railroad cars. On his lunch hour he pretended to get a phone call from the football coach asking him to a special practice that afternoon. The ruse worked, but in the following days Uncle Harry kept calling and asking when Roger would work for the rest of the pay he had received. Roger put him off several times with a variety of excuses, but finally Uncle Harry pinned him down to a Saturday for which he had no ready excuse. Uncle Harry mentioned that he wouldn't be at the yard that day, but his employee Sam would supervise Roger.

During that week Roger thought of how much he didn't want to unload freight cars. Just after he had pushed the dreaded idea of hard work out of his mind, he bumped into Tim. Tim wasn't the brightest boy in the class, but he was good-hearted and fairly strong. Roger told Tim that he was just thinking about him because his uncle needed two strong boys to unload freight cars on Saturday. It was a great chance to impress Uncle Harry, Roger said, because he'd been looking for two boys to work regularly around the yard in the fall. They would be paid pretty well. Tim listened and liked what he heard. He wasn't afraid of work, and, because he knew that Roger's uncle really did own the lumberyard, it seemed like a fine opportunity for him.

Roger told Tim to meet him outside the yard's office wearing heavy shoes and comfortable clothes. On Saturday morning Roger arrived right on time. So did Tim. Roger greeted Tim heartily, approving of his clothing and his shoes. Roger found Sam in the yard's office and introduced Tim, saying that Uncle Harry had asked him to bring a friend to help. Sam then pointed out the railroad cars to unload, and Roger took Tim over and showed him what to do.

Roger told Tim that he should go ahead and start the job. Uncle Harry, who was away, had asked Roger to run an important errand across town. He didn't know how long he'd be, but he'd try to get back as soon as he could. There was a phone in the shed near the railroad spur, and he'd phone Tim and tell him when he would rejoin him on the job.

Roger phoned three times, each time with a story about all he was doing for Uncle Harry. Tim worked on and finally finished unloading the two freight cars at 4:30. Roger still hadn't returned, and Tim was exhausted. He wished Uncle Harry had seen what a good worker he was.

When Uncle Harry came to work on Monday morning, he noted, with some surprise, that the freight cars had been unloaded satisfactorily. He asked Sam if he had noticed Roger working on Saturday. Sam said that he had only seen Roger at 8:30 and not after that.

"Who," Uncle Harry wanted to know, "unloaded those cars?"

"Oh, some nice kid about Roger's age," Sam replied. "Roger said he had cleared it with you."

Name   Date

Roger the Dodger: Student Responses

Think about your answers to the following questions and write your response to each.

1. When Tim asks Roger for his money, what will Roger say?

_____

_____

_____

2. What will Uncle Harry say to Roger?

_____

_____

_____

3. How can you protect yourself against the Rogers of the world?

_____

_____

_____

4. Do you think Uncle Harry tried to learn the whole story? Explain.

_____

_____

_____

For the Teacher

Roger the Dodger
Shirking

The Story

Although some of us find it hard to believe that there are cunning, deceitful individuals such as Roger in the world, we sometimes find out, to our chagrin, that there are. In fact, periodicals are full of stories about fraud in our country. Due to the ease of accessing personal information on the Internet, we have more fraud, such as identity theft, than ever.

The Questions

It's likely that Roger will pay Tim. After all, Tim could make it unpleasant if he doesn't get paid. But whether Roger will give Tim his rightful share is somewhat doubtful. It's Roger's nature to connive, unfortunately.

The most interesting question is the one concerning what Uncle Harry will say to Roger. Uncle Harry has obviously learned that Tim did all the work for Roger, and Uncle Harry isn't the kind of man to shrug his shoulders in cases such as this. Your students may have some good ideas about how Roger will try to wiggle out of this predicament.

It's important for young people to be aware that there are connivers in the world, both young and old. The fact that we have to protect ourselves from con artists is quite sad. Nevertheless, the more information we have about scams and frauds, the better off society will be. So the main way to guard against the con artists is to learn about their tactics. There is currently a nationwide campaign to educate the public about mail fraud, telephone fraud, and fraudulent practices on the Internet.

It is quite likely that Uncle Harry is no fool. He will probably do some checking on his nephew.

An Activity Exploring Fraud

A logical activity to grow out of the reading of "Roger the Dodger" is to look into periodicals and on the Internet for reports of scams and frauds. Many magazines and newspapers are crusading about the numerous scams being perpetrated, with women, the elderly, and the uneducated and/or gullible as targeted victims. *Modern Maturity*, the AARP magazine, has been particularly diligent in reporting every new kind of scam that is reported.

Your students could investigate the subject for one or two weeks by reading newspapers and magazines, and monitoring television and the Internet. They might work individually; or, if you think it more productive, they could work in small groups to ferret out the information.

Incidentally, recently some industry giants have paid hefty fines to the government and made settlements to consumers because of fraudulent practices in advertising, packaging, and pricing. Their willingness to adopt deceitful practices has shocked many people.

A Good Team

Marcus and Tanya were in charge of promoting the big dance and selling tickets for it. Because he was clever at making up slogans and catchy phrases, Marcus was the dance committee's logical choice to write the copy for the posters and the ad for the school newspaper. Because of her enthusiasm and get-up-and-go, Tanya was everyone's choice to help Marcus promote the dance. She would make the announcement at the last assembly, and Marcus would write the script.

They made a good team because Tanya knew Marcus was a good writer, and Marcus knew Tanya would be great in her presentation to the assembly. He knew that she would also be good at cajoling store owners and managers into letting them put his posters in their windows.

The only trouble that occurred between Marcus and Tanya happened on the day before the assembly. Tanya wanted to make her announcement in a jitterbug costume—to highlight the dance's theme—but Marcus thought that she should be more dignified and simply wear the clothes she usually wore. Eventually Tanya talked Marcus into seeing it her way.

After she had made the announcement, Marcus was glad that he had agreed to the costume. It really did help communicate the dance's theme to the students. With posters in almost every store in town, they thought the dance was sure to be a big success.

RESPONSES

A Good Team: Student Responses

Think about your answers to the following questions and write your response to each.

1. Every time two people try to cooperate to do a job, their collaboration is not assured of success. What does it take for two people to cooperate and to succeed? Be specific in your answer.

_____

_____

_____

_____

2. Because their personalities and talents were quite different, was it harder or easier for Tanya and Marcus to work well together? Explain your reasoning.

_____

_____

_____

_____

3. What is the greatest single obstacle of successful cooperation? Why?

_____

_____

_____

4. What is the single most important factor in being able to cooperate successfully?

_____

_____

A Good Team
Cooperation

The Story

The fact that there has been a cooperative learning movement for at least two decades in the United States attests to the faith we place in individuals being able to help each other to achieve goals. As presented in the story, Marcus and Tanya are almost ideally suited to work together in promoting the dance. There really are many times when students can work cooperatively in your classroom if they have a shared goal and aren't self-centered.

The Questions

First, it helps immeasurably for the cooperating parties to have a common goal, one that means something to both of them. Being required to work on someone else's project is not as motivating. Second, cooperation implies that both parties will get something out of the collaboration, but there will be trouble if one or both look at the undertaking selfishly. For example, in raising their chicks, a pair of Adélie penguins has only one objective—to nurture them until they can become independent. Neither mother nor father is concerned about herself or himself during the period when they are raising their chicks. The best cooperative duos are like that.

Personalities often clash when people work closely together. Tanya has the kind of disposition that complements Marcus's. That, of course, is the ideal in cooperative ventures, including marriage.

The biggest single obstacle to cooperation occurs when an individual is primarily concerned with having his or her own way (and therefore doesn't listen to the ideas of others).

Because cooperative learning has been emphasized in schools so much in the past two decades, students likely will have some ideas about this question. They may think that the ability to listen to others and take their needs, skills, and personalities into consideration is a key for cooperating successfully.

An Activity Exploring Cooperation

"Working Together" on page 142 will give your students a chance to delve more deeply into the all-important matter of teamwork and cooperation. Distribute the exercise and have each student do some serious thinking about the items.

For another look at cooperation, ask your students to find two persons in literature who best exemplify the cooperative spirit. Have them restrict their search to only two cooperating characters.

After determining which fictional or nonfictional pair best exemplifies the cooperative spirit, the students should write a justification for their selection, supporting the choice with anecdotes from the book(s). Depending upon your purpose in making this assignment, you might first review the principles of essay writing with your class.

ACTIVITY

Working Together

An activity exploring cooperation

It takes teamwork to win athletic contests such as those in baseball, basketball, hockey, and football. The team with the stars doesn't always win. On many occasions the team with the superior personnel has lost to a team that worked well together. That possibility is what makes team sports especially fascinating. Team sports require teamwork—that is, the team members have to operate as a team, not as individuals.

Put a check next to each of the activities that requires teamwork.

_____ Fighting a flu epidemic

_____ Playing a round of golf

_____ Racing a stock car

_____ Flying an airliner

_____ Removing an appendix

_____ Making a quilt

_____ Doing a crossword puzzle

_____ Preventing the pollution of rivers and lakes

_____ Running a summer camp

_____ Writing a letter

Name   Date

_____ Shoeing a horse

_____ Mending a barbed-wire fence

_____ Designing a dress

_____ Playing a card game

_____ Walking a dog

_____ Campaigning for public office

Choose one of the activities you checked above. Tell why it requires teamwork.

_____

_____

_____

_____

Kristin

Kristin, a small, quiet girl, made Mrs. Morris happiest when she settled into her seat. It wasn't that she was Mrs. Morris's favorite student—she really didn't have a favorite. It was just that the class always seemed to go better when Kristin was present. Something about her attitude concerning school and learning rubbed off on her classmates. And she had a calming effect on Terrell. Early in the year Mrs. Morris had discovered that when this class was learning in groups of four or five, Terrell, who was usually all over the classroom, was a lot less disruptive if he were in a group with Kristin.

It wasn't that Kristin particularly led the group by her ideas; she led more by example. Kristin's way was to get the goals of a lesson clearly in mind and then try to reach those goals by using her time efficiently and thoughtfully. She didn't get the highest grades in the class, but she always did very well because, for any assignment, she anticipated what needed to be done and got it done in a timely fashion. Other students saw this and it inspired them to work in the same way.

Thankfully, thought Mrs. Morris, her fellow students didn't regard Kristin as a "goody-goody." She was pleasant and low-key in her conscientious ways and never said anything to anyone for not doing what he or she was supposed to do.

_____   _____

Name   **Date**

Kristin: Student Responses

Think about your answers to the following questions and write your response to each.

1. What are the reasons for considering someone conscientious?

_____

_____

_____

2. Do you know any student who resembles Kristin? Without naming names, tell why that student is like Kristin.

_____

_____

_____

3. Would you rather have a leader who leads with ideas or a leader who leads by her or his example? Explain.

_____

_____

_____

_____

4. Can a person who is conscientious also be selfish? How?

_____

_____

_____

_____

Kristin
Conscientiousness

The Story

There *was* a Kristin, and she was a joy to be around. Mrs. Morris was generally too concerned with Terrell and other less-well-behaved students to pay a great deal of attention to Kristin, but she was very grateful to have Kristin in her social studies class. She was indeed a bright, charming young lady who was also very conscientious.

The Questions

What does it mean to be conscientious? Most conscientious people have personal standards for performing in satisfactory ways. In addition, they try to do the "right thing." That can mean being on time, fulfilling obligations promptly, recognizing and performing chores or duties readily, anticipating the needs of others, anticipating what should be done next, being thorough and finishing what they start out to do, not needing a lot of supervision, and doing a little extra when it is helpful to do so. Your students might compile a somewhat different set of behaviors, but they'll nail down the most important points.

If a class is lucky, it may have one or two Kristins, but they aren't always girls. This question should probably be answered individually because it might embarrass any Kristins your class could be blessed with.

The third question could require some genuine thinking. At first your students might think that leaders with good ideas are better than those who lead by example, but several studies have revealed that the students with the best ideas are ignored because the ones who have been accustomed to leading naturally take over. In addition, the ones with the best ideas are often the most creative, and they may not be popular, or they may be "put down" for having wild ideas and not conforming.

It is quite possible for a conscientious individual to be selfish. The super-conscientious person may be motivated in ways that relate mainly to himself or herself and that are only tangentially related to others. The two traits are not necessarily correlated, however. Kristin was not overly ego-involved—and so wouldn't be regarded as selfish—when she helped groups accomplish their goals.

An Activity Exploring Conscientiousness

Have students think about their own acts of conscientiousness. What are their own "personal standards" and how do they fulfill their obligations to friends, relatives, schoolwork, or people who employ them to baby-sit or do odd jobs? Hold a class discussion, giving each student a chance to offer his or her own examples.

Bob's Buddy

Bob wasn't very big, but the other kids didn't hassle him. He had a quiet, confident way of dealing with most situations. In contrast, David, who was pale and slightly built, was picked on continually by the boys in the class, and even some boys a year or two younger. Although his mother encouraged David to eat healthy food, particularly vegetables and fruits, he preferred junk food and soft drinks. The two boys weren't much alike in their preferences for activities, either, but somehow they had been friends all during elementary school. In fact, Bob had been the only one in all of that time to defend David when he was picked on by the boys and some of the girls.

Bob ordinarily didn't have to use his fists when he defended David. He only tried to shame David's tormentors and convince them that they were just being mean for no good reason. David was grateful to Bob for intervening through the years. But he became more and more tentative in his interactions with the kids at school. After all, Bob couldn't look after him all the time.

One morning, as the students filed into their classroom, Josh, a big strong boy, jostled David and then in a rough voice said, "Watch where you're going, you jerk!"

For some reason that even he didn't understand, David gave Josh a big push. For a moment Josh was so surprised that he didn't do anything but gawk at David. Then he said, "I'll see you after school, David."

Bob happened to witness the scuffle between David and Josh, but he didn't say anything to David all during the school day. For his part, David was scared silly. He knew what would happen to him when he left the school grounds. Josh, and maybe someone else, would jump on him and pound him. He'd never been so frightened. Should he phone his mother and ask her to leave work and pick him up? No, he couldn't do that.

When the teacher dismissed the class at 3 o'clock, David gathered up his jacket and books and set out for home in a hurry. Maybe he'd get to the gate before Josh did. As David left the building, Bob fell in step with him. "Thought I'd come over to your place and take a stab at your new computer game, David," Bob said casually.

The two boys walked through the gate and to David's house without incident.

Name

Date

Bob's Buddy: Student Responses

Think about your answers to the following questions and write your response to each.

1. How will David show his gratitude to Bob? Will he say anything at all?

_____

_____

_____

2. David is benefiting from his friendship with Bob, but what is Bob getting out of it?

_____

_____

_____

3. What does the saying "A friend in need is a friend indeed" mean?

_____

_____

_____

4. Bullying is getting more attention now than ever before. Why do you think there are so many incidents of bullying in schools?

_____

_____

_____

For the Teacher

Bob's Buddy
Friendship

The Story

"Bob's Buddy" is the story of a weaker boy being protected by his stronger friend. Every year there are probably several similar incidents in your school. Fortunately, strong boys become friends with boys who are liable to be picked on. As is hinted at in the second question following the story, both parties benefit from the relationship.

David's surprising reaction to being shoved is not unusual in boys who have been bullied continually. Occasionally they flare up because it gets to be too much for them to take. On rare occasions they strike back and the astounded tormentor lets it go at that. In the case of David and Josh, however, there was likely to be some retaliation. Bob prevented that.

The Questions

David may or may not acknowledge that Bob has saved him from a pummeling. Often there is an unspoken understanding among friends in situations such as this one when an incident is embarrassing for one of the friends. Bob has simply prevented what would have been an unfair altercation by accompanying David home.

The friend who is stronger by virtue of physical strength, intellectual prowess, or social skills benefits from helping a weaker friend for rather obvious reasons. He or she has the satisfaction of knowing that he or she has done a good deed and really helped the friend. Whether the appreciation is expressed aloud or merely understood, the stronger friend feels good about it, and the friendship between the two is strengthened.

The third question is meant to reinforce the idea that friends help each other. However, it has always seemed to us that the old maxim is badly put—it's the one who helps, not the one who needs help, who is being a true friend.

It is likely that the question about bullying will get quite a reaction from students. Maybe they have some notions about why there seems to be an epidemic of bullying throughout the country.

An Activity Exploring Friendship

We form friendships by associating with others in work, play, social gatherings, and voluntary and involuntary groups (classes in school being most prominent for youngsters). First there must be contact between two or more individuals, and then the contact must continue. In "When Acquaintances Become Friends" on page 152, your students are to give their own choices for the best situations in which friendships can flower. This is a purely subjective matter, of course. The purpose of the exercise is simply to get your students thinking about the friendships that they have formed and the circumstances in which the friendships grew out of acquaintanceships.

We regularly refer to people we know as "friends," but friendship means more than recognizing, greeting, and speaking with someone occasionally. A friend is someone we can depend upon to help in some way when there is a need, and "When Acquaintances Become Friends" offers students a chance to recognize this point.

ACTIVITY

_____   _____
          Name   **Date**

When Acquaintances Become Friends

An activity exploring friendship

Consider each of the three general situations given below, and then decide which would be the best occasion for turning an acquaintanceship into a friendship.

1. Activities you can do alone or with someone:

running	walking or hiking
boating	swimming
skateboarding	playing hopscotch
skipping rope	skiing
skating	

Which of the activities listed would be the best to do with an acquaintance who might become a friend? Why would it be the best?

_____

_____

Tell how it could happen.

_____

_____

Name   Date

2. Activities in which teams compete:

hockey	football
wrestling	baseball or softball
basketball	volleyball
track and field	soccer

Which of these activities would be best to do with an acquaintance who might become a friend? Why would it be the best of those sports listed?

_____

_____

Tell how it could happen.

_____

_____

_____

3. Social gatherings or youth activities:

church youth group	after-school club
YMCA/YWCA	Boys and Girls Club
Boys Scouts/Girl Scouts	neighborhood gang
summer camp	

Which activity would be best for developing a friendship? Why?

_____

_____

Tell how it could happen.

_____

_____

_____

D–E

decisions, making quick (activity), 127–128
dependability, 66–71. *See also* reliability
    case study, 66–67
    student activity, 70–71
    teacher guide, 69
    work sheet, 68
dishonesty, 15–20. *See also* honesty
    case study, 15
    student activity, 19–20
    teacher guide, 17–18
    work sheet, 16
embarrassment, 13–14

F

fairness, 90–95. *See also* unfairness
    case study, 90–91
    student activity, 94–95
    teacher guide, 93
    work sheet, 92
FRIENDSHIP, 147–153
    case study, 147–148
    student activity, 152–153
    teacher guide, 150–151
    work sheet, 149

G

generosity, 48–51. *See also* greed; stinginess
    case study, 48–49
    student activity, 51
    teacher guide, 51
    work sheet, 50
GOODWILL, 90–112
    fairness, 90–95
    gratitude, 103–108
    ingratitude, 109–112
    unfairness, 96–102
grateful, feeling (activity), 107–108
gratitude, 103–108. *See also* ingratitude
    case study, 103–104
    student activity, 107–108
    teacher guide, 106
    work sheet, 105
greed, 52–57. *See also* generosity; stinginess
    case study, 52–53
    student activity, 56–57
    teacher guide, 55
    work sheet, 54

H

hoarding, 61
honesty, 9–14. *See also* dishonesty
    case study, 9–10
    student activity, 13–14
    teacher guide, 12
    work sheet, 11
hypocrisy (activity), 36

I

INDUSTRIOUSNESS, 129–138
    persistence, 129–134
    shirking, 135–138
ingratitude, 109–112. *See also* gratitude
    case study, 109–110
    student activity, 112
    teacher guide, 112
    work sheet, 111
insincerity, 32–36. *See also* sincerity
    case study, 32–33
    student activity, 36
    teacher guide, 35
    work sheet, 34
INTEGRITY, 3–36
    cheating, 21–25
    dishonesty, 15–20
    honesty, 9–14
    insincerity, 32–36
    sincerity, 26–31
    truthfulness, 3–8
Internet scams and frauds (activity), 138

K

KINDNESS, 37–61
    generosity, 48–51
    greed, 52–57
    kindness, 37–42
    stinginess, 58–61
    unkindness, 43–47
kindness, 37–42. *See also* unkindness
    case study, 37–38
    student activity, 41–42
    teacher guide, 40
    work sheet, 39

M–N

mistakes, owning up to, 5
name-calling (activity), 47
new teacher, being open-minded about, 117–120